LOCO

SIXTY-FOURTH EDITION
2022

The complete guide to all
Locomotives which operate on
the national railway
and Eurotunnel networks

Robert Pritchard

ISBN 978 1909 431 71 3

© 2021. Platform 5 Publishing Ltd, 52 Broadfield Road, Sheffield, S8 0XJ,
England.

Printed in England by The Lavenham Press, Lavenham, Suffolk.

CONTENTS

Provision of information 2
Updates 2
Britain's Railway System 3
Introduction...13
General Information 15
1.1. Diesel Shunting Locomotives..20
1.2. Main Line Diesel Locomotives..27
2. Electro-Diesel & Electric Locomotives 81
3. Eurotunnel Locomotives 91
4. Locomotives Awaiting Disposal..94
5. Locomotives Exported For Use Abroad....................................95
6. Codes...98

PROVISION OF INFORMATION

This book has been compiled with care to be as accurate as possible, but some information is not easily available and the publisher cannot be held responsible for any errors or omissions. We would like to thank the companies and individuals who have been helpful in supplying information to us. The authors of this series of books are always pleased to receive notification of any inaccuracies that may be found, to enhance future editions. Please send comments to:

Robert Pritchard, Platform 5 Publishing Ltd, 52 Broadfield Road, Sheffield, S8 0XJ, England.

e-mail: robert.pritchard@platform5.com   **Tel:** 0114 255 2625.

This book is updated to information received by 11 October 2021.

UPDATES

This book is updated to the Stock Changes given in **Today's Railways UK 237** (November 2021). The Platform 5 railway magazine **"Today's Railways UK"** publishes Stock Changes every month to update this book. The magazine also contains news and rolling stock information on the railways of Great Britain and is published on the second Monday of every month. For further details of **Today's Railways UK**, please contact Platform 5 Publishing Ltd or visit our website **www.platform5.com**.

Front cover photograph: Colas Rail-liveried 70801 is seen near Armathwaite with 6J37 12.58 Carlisle–Chirk loaded timber on 10 August 2021.   **Andrew Mason**

BRITAIN'S RAILWAY SYSTEM

The structure of Britain's railway system has changed significantly during 2020–21, following the ongoing Covid-19 pandemic which saw passenger numbers drop by around 60–70% across the country. Although passengers started to return in larger numbers during 2021, this original drop in numbers meant that franchises were no longer profitable and the Government was forced to step in and provide financial support to operators. Initially in March 2020 the Transport Secretary suspended rail franchising and operators transitioned to "Emergency Measures Agreements". These EMAs suspended the normal financial agreements, instead transferring all revenue and cost risk to the Government. The existing operators in England all accepted these new arrangements and continued to operate trains (initially with reduced service frequencies) for a small management fee. Similar arrangements were put in place by the Scottish and Welsh Governments for ScotRail, Caledonian Sleeper and Transport for Wales.

The EMAs initially lasted for six months until September 2020, from which time longer "Emergency Recovery Management Agreements" (ERMAs) were put in place. These were similar management contracts which continued to see operators run services for a management fee. Whilst some operators are still running under ERMAs, others are transitioning to new National Rail Contracts (NRCs). During the NRC operators are paid a fixed management fee of around 1.5% for operating services and additional small performance fees if agreed targets are achieved.

In the longer term a new body called Great British Railways will take over the running of the railways and specifically take over Network Rail's responsibilities as well as some functions currently carried out by the Department for Transport and Rail Delivery Group. The franchise model will be changed to one of concessions, although this will take some years to fully implement.

In London and on Merseyside concessions were already in place. These see the operator paid a fee to run the service, usually within tightly specified guidelines. Operators running a concession would not normally take commercial risks, although there are usually penalties and rewards in the contract.

Britain's national railway infrastructure is currently owned by a "not for dividend" company, Network Rail. In 2014 Network Rail was reclassified as a public sector company, being described by the Government as a "public sector arm's-length body of the Department for Transport".

Most stations and maintenance depots are leased to and operated by the Train Operating Companies (TOCs), but some larger stations are controlled by Network Rail. The only exception is the infrastructure on the Isle of Wight: The Island Line franchise uniquely included maintenance of the infrastructure as well as the operation of passenger services. Both the infrastructure and trains are operated by South Western Railway.

Trains are operated by TOCs over Network Rail tracks (the National Network), regulated by access agreements between the parties involved. In general,

TOCs are responsible for the provision and maintenance of the trains and staff necessary for the direct operation of services, whilst Network Rail is responsible for the provision and maintenance of the infrastructure and also for staff to regulate the operation of services.

The Department for Transport (DfT) is the authority for the national network. Transport Scotland oversees the award of the ScotRail and Caledonian Sleeper franchises and in April 2022 will take over the operation of the ScotRail franchise from Abellio. In February 2021 the Welsh Government took over the operation of the Wales & Borders franchise from KeolisAmey.

Each franchise was set up with the right to run specified services within a specified area for a period of time, in return for the right to charge fares and, where appropriate, to receive financial support from the Government. Subsidy was payable in respect of socially necessary services. Service standards are monitored by the DfT throughout the duration of the franchise. Franchisees earned revenue primarily from fares and from subsidy. They generally leased stations from Network Rail and earned rental income by sub-letting parts of them, for example to retailers.

TOC's and open access operator's main costs are the track access charges they pay to Network Rail, the costs of leasing stations and rolling stock and of employing staff. Franchisees may do light maintenance work on rolling stock or contract it out to other companies. Heavy maintenance is normally carried out by the Rolling Stock Leasing Companies, according to contracts.

Note that a railway "reporting period" is four weeks.

DOMESTIC PASSENGER TRAIN OPERATORS

The majority of passenger trains are operated by Train Operating Companies, now supported by the Government through the Emergency Recovery Management Agreements, which have replaced franchises. Some operators are now transitioning to new National Rail Contracts. Caledonian Sleeper and ScotRail are still operating under Emergency Measures Agreements (EMAs). For reference the date of the expiry of the original franchise is also given here (if later than the current ERMA or NRC expiry date).

Name of franchise	Operator	Trading Name
Caledonian Sleeper	Serco	**Caledonian Sleeper**

EMA until 31 December 2021; original franchise was until 31 March 2030

The Sleeper franchise started in April 2015 when operation of the ScotRail and ScotRail Sleeper franchises was separated. Abellio won the ScotRail and Serco the Caledonian Sleeper franchise. Caledonian Sleeper operates four trains nightly between London Euston and Scotland using locomotives hired from GBRf. New CAF Mark 5 rolling stock was introduced during 2019.

Chiltern	Arriva (Deutsche Bahn)	**Chiltern Railways**

EMRA until 11 December 2021, the original franchise expiry date

Chiltern Railways operates a frequent service between London Marylebone, Oxford, Banbury and Birmingham Snow Hill, with some peak trains extending to Kidderminster. There are also regular services from Marylebone to Stratford-upon-Avon and to Aylesbury Vale Parkway via Amersham (along the London Underground Metropolitan Line). The fleet consists of DMUs of Classes 165, and 168 plus a number of locomotive-hauled rakes used on some of the Birmingham and Oxford route trains, worked by Class 68s hired from DRS.

| **Cross Country** | Arriva (Deutsche Bahn) | **CrossCountry** |

ERMA until 15 October 2023

CrossCountry operates a network of long distance services between Scotland, the North-East of England and Manchester to the South-West of England, Reading, Southampton, Bournemouth and Guildford, centred on Birmingham New Street. These trains are mainly formed of diesel Class 220/221 Voyagers, supplemented by a small number of HSTs on the NE–SW route. Inter-urban services also link Nottingham, Leicester and Stansted Airport with Birmingham and Cardiff. These trains use Class 170 DMUs.

| **Crossrail** | MTR | **TfL Rail** |

Concession until 27 May 2023 (with an option to extend the concession by 2 years to May 2025)

This concession started in May 2015. Initially Crossrail took over the Liverpool Street–Shenfield stopping service from Greater Anglia, using a fleet of Class 315 EMUs, with the service branded "TfL Rail". New Class 345 EMUs are being introduced on this route and are also now used between Paddington and Hayes & Harlington, Heathrow Airport and Reading. TfL Rail currently also operates the former Heathrow Connect stopping service that now also uses Class 345s. The opening of Crossrail through central London has been delayed and operation through new tunnels beneath central London, from Shenfield and Abbey Wood in the east to Reading and Heathrow Airport in the west is now expected spring 2022. It will then be branded the "Elizabeth Line".

| **East Coast** | DfT | **London North Eastern Railway** |

Operated by DfT's "Operator of Last Resort" until June 2023 (with an option to extend by 2 years to June 2025)

LNER operates frequent long distance trains on the East Coast Main Line between London King's Cross, Leeds, Lincoln, Harrogate, York, Newcastle-upon-Tyne and Edinburgh, with less frequent services to Bradford, Skipton, Hull, Glasgow, Stirling, Aberdeen and Inverness. A new fleet of 65 Hitachi Class 800 and 801 "Azuma" trains have all now been introduced (these are a mix of bi-mode and electric, 5- and 9-car units) and operate the majority of services. A small number of Class 91+Mark 4 sets have been retained until at least 2023 and are mainly used on Leeds and York services.

| **East Midlands** | Abellio | **East Midlands Railway** |

ERMA until 31 March 2022; original franchise was until 21 August 2027

EMR operates a mix of long distance high speed services on the Midland Main Line (MML), from London St Pancras to Sheffield (with one peak-hour train to Leeds), Nottingham (plus peak-hour trains to Lincoln) and Corby, and local and regional services ranging from the long distance Norwich–Liverpool route to Nottingham–Skegness, Nottingham–Mansfield–Worksop, Newark–Matlock and Derby–Crewe. It also operates local services across Lincolnshire. Trains on the MML are worked by a fleet of Class 180 and 222 DMUs, whilst the local and regional fleet consists of DMU Classes 153, 156, 158 and 170. Class 360 EMUs started to operate services on the newly electrified St Pancras–Corby route from May 2021.

| **East Anglia** | Abellio (Netherlands Railways) (60%)/Mitsui Group (40%) | **Greater Anglia** |

NRC until 19 September 2024 with option for a 2 year extension; original franchise was until 11 October 2025

Greater Anglia operates main line trains between London Liverpool Street, Ipswich and Norwich and local trains across Norfolk, Suffolk and parts of Cambridgeshire. It also runs local and commuter services into Liverpool Street from the Great Eastern (including Southend, Braintree and Clacton) and West Anglia (including Ely/Cambridge and Stansted Airport) routes. In 2019–20 a new fleet of Stadler EMUs and bi-mode EMUs (Classes 745 and 755) was introduced on the GEML and in East Anglia, replacing older DMUs and loco-hauled trains. Classes 317, 321, 322 and 379 EMUs are still operated out of Liverpool Street and during 2020–22 are being replaced by a large fleet of 133 new Class 720 Aventras.

Essex Thameside   Trenitalia   **c2c**
NRC until 25 July 2023; original franchise was until 10 November 2029

c2c operates an intensive, principally commuter, service from London Fenchurch Street to Southend and Shoeburyness, via both Upminster and Tilbury. The fleet consists of 74 Class 357 EMUs, with 12 Class 720 Aventras on order.

Great Western   First Group   **Great Western Railway**
EMA until 25 June 2022; original franchise was until 31 March 2023. New Direct Award being negotiated for a further 3 years + an optional extra 3 years

Great Western Railway operates long distance trains from London Paddington to South Wales, the West Country and Worcester and Hereford. In addition there are frequent trains along the Thames Valley corridor to Newbury/Bedwyn and Oxford, plus local and regional trains throughout the South-West including the Cornish, Devon and Thames Valley branches, the Reading–Gatwick North Downs Line and Cardiff–Portsmouth Harbour and Bristol–Weymouth regional routes. Long distance services are in the hands of a fleet of Class 800/802 bi-mode InterCity Express Trains. DMUs of Classes 165 and 166 are used on the Thames Valley branches and North Downs routes as well as on local services around Bristol and Exeter and across to Cardiff. Class 387 EMUs are used between Paddington, Reading, Didcot Parkway and Newbury. Classes 150, 158, 165 and 166 and a fleet of short 4-car HSTs are used on local and regional trains in the South-West. A small fleet of Class 57s is maintained to work the overnight "Cornish Riviera" Sleeper service between London Paddington and Penzance formed of Mark 3 coaches. In 2021–22 tri-mode Class 769 units will be introduced on some routes around Reading.

London Rail   Arriva (Deutsche Bahn)   **London Overground**
Concession until 25 May 2024 (with an option to extend the concession by 2 years to May 2026)

London Overground operates services on the Richmond–Stratford North London Line and the Willesden Junction–Clapham Junction West London Line, plus the East London Line from Highbury & Islington to New Cross and New Cross Gate, with extensions to Clapham Junction (via Denmark Hill), Crystal Palace and West Croydon. It also runs services from London Euston to Watford Junction. All these use Class 378 EMUs, with new Class 710s also recently introduced onto the Watford Junction route. Class 710s also operate services on the Gospel Oak–Barking line. London Overground also operates some suburban services from London Liverpool Street – to Chingford, Enfield Town and Cheshunt. These services all use Class 710s, with one unit also used on the Romford–Upminster shuttle.

Merseyrail Electrics   Serco (50%)/Abellio (Netherlands Railways) (50%)   **Merseyrail**
Concession until 22 July 2028. Under the control of Merseytravel PTE instead of the DfT Due to be reviewed every five years to fit in with the Merseyside Local Transport Plan

Merseyrail operates services between Liverpool and Southport, Ormskirk, Kirkby, Hunts Cross, New Brighton, West Kirby, Chester and Ellesmere Port, using Class 507 and 508 EMUs. A new fleet of Class 777 EMUs will be introduced in 2022–23.

| **Northern** | DfT | **Northern** |

Operated by DfT's "Operator of Last Resort" until further notice

Northern operates a range of inter-urban, commuter and rural services throughout the North of England, including those around the cities of Leeds, Manchester, Sheffield, Liverpool and Newcastle. The network extends from Chathill in the north to Nottingham in the south, and Cleethorpes in the east to St Bees in the west. Long distance services include Leeds–Carlisle, Morpeth–Carlisle and York–Blackpool North. The operator uses a large fleet of DMUs of Classes 150, 153, 155, 156, 158, 170 and 195 plus EMU Classes 319, 323, 331 and 333. The new fleets of DMUs (Class 195) and EMUs (Class 331) have now been introduced on a number of routes, and were followed by Class 769 bi-mode diesel electric units (converted from Class 319s) in 2021.

| **ScotRail** | Abellio (Netherlands Railways) | **ScotRail** |

EMA until 31 December 2021; original franchise was until 31 March 2022. From 1 April 2022 the Scottish Government will take over the operation of the franchise.

ScotRail provides almost all passenger services within Scotland and also trains from Glasgow to Carlisle via Dumfries, some of which extend to Newcastle-upon-Tyne (jointly operated with Northern). The company operates a large fleet of DMUs of Classes 156, 158 and 170 and EMU Classes 318, 320, 334, 380 and 385. A fleet of 25 refurbished HSTs are being introduced onto InterCity services between Edinburgh/Glasgow and Aberdeen and Inverness and also between Inverness and Aberdeen. In 2021 five Class 153s were also introduced on the West Highland Line (Oban line) to provide more capacity and space for bikes and other luggage.

| **South Eastern** | DfT | **Southeastern** |

Operated by DfT's "Operator of Last Resort" from 17 October 2021 until further notice. Govia was stripped of the franchise following a breach of its franchise commitment.

Southeastern operates all services in the south-east London suburbs, the whole of Kent and part of Sussex, which are primarily commuter services to London. It also operates domestic High Speed trains on HS1 from London St Pancras to Ashford, Ramsgate, Dover and Faversham with additional peak services on other routes. EMUs of Classes 375, 376, 377, 465 and 466 are used, along with Class 395s on the High Speed lines. In 2021–22 the 30 Class 707 EMUs, sub-leased from South Western Railway, are also being introduced.

| **South Western** | First Group (70%)/MTR (30%) | **South Western Railway** |

NRC until 30 May 2023 with option for a 2 year extension; original franchise ran until 17 August 2024

South Western Railway operates trains from London Waterloo to destinations across the South and South-West including Woking, Basingstoke, Southampton, Portsmouth, Salisbury, Exeter, Reading and Weymouth, as well as suburban services from Waterloo. SWR also runs services between Ryde and Shanklin on the Isle of Wight, from November 2021 using a fleet of five third rail Vivarail Class 484 units (converted former LU D78 stock). The rest of the fleet consists of DMU Classes 158 and 159 and EMU Classes 444, 450, 455, 456, 458 and 707. A new fleet of Bombardier Class 701s are being delivered to replace Classes 455, 456 and 707 in 2021–22.

| **Thameslink, Southern & Great Northern (TSGN)** | Govia (Go-Ahead/Keolis) | **Govia Thameslink Railway** |

ERMA until 31 March 2022

TSGN is the largest operator in Great Britain (the former Southern franchise was combined with Thameslink/Great Northern in 2015). GTR uses four brands: "Thameslink" for trains between Cambridge North, Peterborough, Bedford and Rainham, Sevenoaks, East Grinstead,

Brighton, Littlehampton and Horsham via central London and also on the Sutton/Wimbledon loop using Class 700 EMUs. "Great Northern" comprises services from London King's Cross and Moorgate to Welwyn Garden City, Hertford North, Peterborough, Cambridge and King's Lynn using Class 387 and 717 EMUs. "Southern" operates predominantly commuter services between London, Surrey and Sussex and "metro" services in South London, as well as services along the south Coast between Southampton, Brighton, Hastings and Ashford, plus the cross-London service from South Croydon to Milton Keynes. Class 171 DMUs are used on Ashford–Eastbourne and London Bridge–Uckfield services, whilst all other services are in the hands of Class 313, 377, 455 and 700 EMUs. Finally, Gatwick Express operates non-stop trains between London Victoria, Gatwick Airport and Brighton using Class 387/2 EMUs.

| **Trans-Pennine Express** | First Group | **TransPennine Express** |

NRC until 30 May 2023 with option for a 2 year extension

TransPennine Express operates predominantly long distance inter-urban services linking major cities across the North of England, along with Edinburgh and Glasgow in Scotland. The main services are Manchester Airport–Redcar Central, Manchester Piccadilly–Hull, Liverpool–York–Scarborough and Liverpool–Newcastle/Edinburgh along the North Trans-Pennine route via Huddersfield, Leeds and York, and Manchester Piccadilly–Cleethorpes along the South Trans-Pennine route via Sheffield. TPE also operates Manchester Airport–Edinburgh/Glasgow and Liverpool–Glasgow. The fleet consists of Class 185 DMUs, plus three new fleets: Class 68s+Mark 5A sets being used, or to be used, on Liverpool–Scarborough and Manchester Airport–Redcar Central, Class 397s used on Manchester Airport/Liverpool–Scotland and Class 802 bi-mode units used on Liverpool–Newcastle/Edinburgh.

| **Wales & Borders** | Welsh Government | **Transport for Wales** |

From 7 February 2021 the Welsh Government will take direct control of rail service operation. Infrastructure management is continued to be managed by KeolisAmey.

Transport for Wales was procured by the Welsh Government and operates a mix of long distance, regional and local services throughout Wales, including the Valley Lines network of lines around Cardiff, and also through services to the English border counties and to Manchester and Birmingham. The fleet consists of DMUs of Classes 150, 153, 158, 170 and 175 and three locomotive-hauled Mark 4 sets hauled by Class 67s on the Cardiff–Holyhead route. Rebuilt Class 230 D-Trains are to be introduced on the Wrexham–Bidston line in 2021–22 and new Stadler and CAF fleets will be introduced across other routes from 2022.

| **West Coast Partnership** | First Group (70%)/Trenitalia (30%) | **Avanti West Coast** |

ERMA until 15 October 2022; original franchise ran until 31 March 2031. New Direct Award being negotiated for upto 10 years

Avanti West Coast operates long distance services along the West Coast Main Line from London Euston to Birmingham/Wolverhampton, Manchester, Liverpool, Blackpool North and Glasgow using Class 390 Pendolino EMUs. It also operates Class 221 Voyagers on the Euston–Chester–Holyhead route and a small number of trains from Wolverhampton to Shrewsbury and to Wrexham, whilst a mix of Class 221s and 390s are used on the Euston–Birmingham–Glasgow/Edinburgh route.

| **West Midlands Trains** | Abellio (70%)/JR East (15%)/Mitsui (15%) | **West Midlands Railway/ London Northwestern** |

NRC until 19 September 2024 with option for a 2 year extension; original franchise ran until 31 March 2026

West Midlands Trains operates services under two brand names. West Midlands Railway trains are local and regional services around Birmingham, including to Stratford-upon-Avon,

Worcester, Hereford, Redditch, Rugeley and Shrewsbury. WMR is managed by a consortium of 16 councils and the Department for Transport. London Northwestern is the brand used for long distance and regional services from London Euston to Northampton and Birmingham/Crewe and also between Birmingham and Liverpool, Bedford–Bletchley and Watford Junction–St Albans Abbey. The fleet consists of DMU Classes 139, 170 and 172 and EMU Classes 319, 323 and 350. Class 230 D-Trains were introduced onto the Bedford–Bletchley route in 2019 and a new fleet CAF Class 196 DMUs and Bombardier Class 730 EMUs will be introduced on a number of routes from 2022.

NON-FRANCHISED SERVICES

The following operators run non-franchised, or "open access" services (* special seasonal services):

Operator	Trading Name	Route
Heathrow Airport Holdings	Heathrow Express	London Paddington–Heathrow Airport

Heathrow Express is a frequent express passenger service between London Paddington and Heathrow Airport using a sub-fleet of Great Western Railway Class 387 EMUs (now operated jointly with GWR as part of its franchise).

Hull Trains (part of First)	Hull Trains	London King's Cross–Hull

Hull Trains operates six trains a day on weekdays from Hull to London King's Cross via the East Coast Main Line. New bi-mode Class 802s were introduced in 2019–20, replacing the Class 180 DMUs. Two trains in each direction start back from and extend to Beverley.

Grand Central (part of Arriva)	Grand Central	London King's Cross–Sunderland/Bradford Interchange

Grand Central operates four trains a day from Sunderland and four from Bradford Interchange to London King's Cross using Class 180 DMUs.

Locomotive Services (TOC)	Locomotive Services	

Locomotive Services runs various excursions across the network using diesel, electric and steam locomotives operating under the brands Saphos Trains (principally steam-hauled trips), Statesman Rail (diesel-locomotive hauled trips and land cruises), Rail Charter Services (regular seasonal HSTs over the Settle & Carlisle Line), Midland Pullman (HST tours) and Intercity (electric locomotive-hauled tours).

First East Coast	Lumo	London King's Cross–Edinburgh

Lumo started operating services from London to Edinburgh via the East Coast Main Line in October 2021 and from early 2022 will be running five trains per day using new electric Class 803 units.

| North Yorkshire Moors Railway Enterprises | North Yorkshire Moors Railway | Pickering–Grosmont–Whitby/ Battersby, Sheringham–Cromer* |

The North Yorkshire Moors Railway operates services on the national network between Grosmont and Whitby or Grosmont and Battersby as an extension of its Pickering–Grosmont services and also operates services between Sheringham and Cromer on behalf of the North Norfolk Railway.

| South Yorkshire Supertram | Stagecoach Supertram | Meadowhall South–Rotherham Parkgate |

South Yorkshire Supertram holds a passenger licence to allow the operation of the pilot tram-train service linking Sheffield city centre with Rotherham Central and Rotherham Parkgate.

| Tyne & Wear PTE | Tyne & Wear Metro | Pelaw–Sunderland |

Tyne & Wear Passenger Transport Executive holds a passenger license to allow the operation of its Metro service over Network Rail tracks between Pelaw and Sunderland.

| Vintage Trains | Vintage Trains | Birmingham Snow Hill–Stratford-upon-Avon* |

Vintage Trains operates steam-hauled services on a seasonal basis.

| West Coast Railway Company | West Coast Railway Company | Fort William–Mallaig* York–Settle–Carlisle* Carnforth–York–Scarborough* |

WCRC operates steam-hauled services on these routes on a seasonal basis and a range of other excursions across the network, including the Northern Belle luxury train.

INTERNATIONAL PASSENGER OPERATORS

Eurostar International operates passenger services between London St Pancras and mainland Europe. The company, established in 2010, is jointly owned by SNCF (the national operator of France): 55%, SNCB (the national operator of Belgium): 5% and Patina Rail: 40%. Patina Rail is made up of Canadian-based Caisse de dépôt et placement du Québec (CDPG) and UK-based Hermes Infrastructure (owning 30% and 10% respectively). This 40% was previously owned by the UK Government until it was sold in 2015.

In addition, a service for the conveyance of accompanied road vehicles through the Channel Tunnel is provided by the tunnel operating company, Eurotunnel. All Eurotunnel services are operated in top-and-tail mode by the powerful Class 9 Bo-Bo-Bo locomotives.

FREIGHT TRAIN OPERATORS

The following operators operate freight services or empty passenger stock workings under "Open Access" arrangements:

Colas Rail: Colas Rail operates a number of On-Track Machines and also supplies infrastructure monitoring trains for Network Rail. It also operates a number of different freight flows, including oil and timber. Colas Rail has a small but varied fleet consisting of Class 37s, 56s, 66s, 67s and 70s. It also uses HST power cars (Class 43) on some Network Rail test trains.

DB Cargo (UK): Still the biggest freight operator in the country, DBC (EWS until bought by Deutsche Bahn, when it was initially called DB Schenker) provides a large number of infrastructure trains to Network Rail and also operates coal, steel, intermodal and aggregate trains nationwide. The core fleet is Class 66s. Of the original 250 ordered, 79 moved to DB's French and Polish operations, although some of the French locos do return to the UK when major maintenance is required. Around 20 Class 60s are also used on heavier trains, the remainder of the fleet having been stored or sold, although DB Cargo is still responsible for the maintenance of GBRf and DCR Class 60s at Toton.

DBC's fleet of Class 67s are used on passenger or standby duties for Transport for Wales and LNER and also on excursions or special trains. Class 90s see some use on West Coast Main Line freight traffic. The Class 92s are mainly used on a limited number of overnight freights on High Speed 1.

DBC also operates the Class 325 EMUs for Royal Mail and a number of excursion trains.

Devon & Cornwall Railways (part of Cappagh Construction Contractors (London)): DCRail specialises in short-term freight haulage contracts, using Class 56s or four Class 60s acquired from DB Cargo.

Direct Rail Services: DRS has built on its original nuclear flask traffic to operate a number of different services. The main flows are intermodal plus the provision of crews and locomotives to Network Rail for autumn RailHead Treatment Trains and also infrastructure trains. DRS has a varied fleet of locomotives, with Class 20s, 37s, 57s and 66s working alongside the more modern Class 68s and diesel-electric Class 88s. Class 68s are hired to Chiltern Railways and TransPennine Express for passenger work. Its Class 68s are also used on some excursion work.

Freightliner: Freightliner (owned by Genesee & Wyoming) operates container trains from the main Ports at Southampton, Felixstowe, Tilbury and Thamesport to major cities including London, Manchester, Leeds and Birmingham. It also operates trains of coal, cement, infrastructure and aggregates. Most services are worked by Class 66s, with Class 70s mainly used on some of the heavier intermodal trains and cement trains from the Peak District. A small fleet of Class 90 electrics are used on intermodal trains on the Great Eastern and West Coast Main Lines. The Class 90 fleet includes 13 locomotives previously operated by Greater Anglia.

The six Class 59/2s were purchased from DB Cargo and are used alongside the Mendip Rail 59/0s and 59/1s on stone traffic from the Mendip quarries and around the South-East.

GB Railfreight: GBRf (owned by Infracapital) operates a mixture of traffic types, mainly using Class 66s together with a small fleet of Class 73s on infrastructure duties and test trains in the South-East and ten Class 60s acquired from Colas Rail in 2018. The company has also now purchased a number of Class 56s and owns a single Class 59, 59003. Some of the Class 56s are being rebuilt as Class 69s with a new GM engine. A fleet of Class 92s is also used on some intermodal flows to and from Dollands Moor or through the Channel Tunnel to Calais. Traffic includes coal, intermodal, biomass, aggregates and gypsum as well as infrastructure services for Network Rail and London Underground. GBRf also supplies Class 73/9s and Class 92s to Caledonian Sleeper and owns the three former Colas Rail Class 47s.

GBRf also operates some excursion trains, including those using the preserved Class 201 "Hastings" DEMU.

LORAM (UK): LORAM has a freight license and operates a limited number of trains, most hauling On-Track Machines using hired-in locomotives.

Rail Operations Group: This company mainly facilitates rolling stock movements by providing drivers or using locomotives hired from other companies or by using its own fleet of Class 47s or Class 37s hired from Europhoenix or Class 57s hired from DRS. It will also start operating a parcels logistics service using Class 319 units (rebuilt as Class 326 EMUs and Class 768 bi-modes) under its **Orion** subsidiary. ROG also operates test trains for Data Acquisition & Testing Services.

West Coast Railway Company: WCRC has a freight licence but doesn't operate any freight as such – only empty stock movements. Its fleet of Class 47s, supplemented by a smaller number of Class 33s, 37s and 57s, is used on excursion work nationwide.

In addition, Amey, Balfour Beatty Rail, Harsco Rail, Swietelsky Babcock Rail (SB Rail) and VolkerRail operate trains formed of On-Track Machines.

INTRODUCTION

This book contains details of all locomotives which can run on Britain's national railway network, plus those of Eurotunnel.

Locomotives currently approved for use on the national railway network fall into four broad types: passenger, freight, mixed traffic and shunting.

Passenger
The number of dedicated passenger locomotives has not changed significantly in recent years. Classes 43 (HST) and 91 and some members of Classes 57, 67, 68, 73/9 and 92 are dedicated to franchised and Open Access passenger operations. Excursion trains have a few dedicated locomotives but mainly use locomotives that are best described as mixed traffic.

Freight
By far the most numerous locomotives are those used solely for bulk commodity and intermodal freight. Since 1998 a large number of new Class 66 locomotives have replaced many former BR designs and in more recent years smaller numbers of Class 70s have also been introduced. There are however a significant number of BR era Class 20, 37, 47, 56, 60, 73/1, 86, 90 and 92 locomotives still in use; their number has increased slightly as some locomotives have been reinstated to cope with demand. In addition there is a small fleet of Class 59s acquired privately in the 1980s and 1990s and a small number of re-engined Class 57s in use.

Mixed Traffic
In addition to their use on passenger and commodity freight workings these locomotives are used for stock movements and specialist infrastructure and test trains. The majority, but not all, are fitted with Electric Train Supply. Locomotives from Classes 20, 33, 37, 47, 57, 67, 68, 73/9, 88 and 90 fall into this category. Also included under this heading are preserved locomotives permitted to operate on the national railway network. Although these have in the past solely operated excursion trains they are increasingly seeing occasional use on other types of trains. Some, such as Class 50s with GB Railfreight, are frequently used by the main freight companies.

Shunting
Very few shunting locomotives are now permitted to operate freely on the National Railway network. The small number that are have to be fitted with a plethora of safety equipment in order to have engineering acceptance. They are mainly used for local workings such as trips between yards or stock movements between depots and stations. Otherwise, shunting locomotives are not permitted to venture from depots or yards onto the National Railway network other than into defined limits within interface infrastructure. Remotely-controlled driverless shunters are not included in this book. However, all ex-BR shunting locomotives are listed under Section 1.1 "Diesel Shunting Locomotives".

Locomotives which are owned by, for example, DB Cargo or Freightliner, which have been withdrawn from service and are awaiting disposal are listed in the main part of the book. Locomotives which are awaiting disposal at scrapyards are listed in the "Locomotives Awaiting Disposal" section.

Only preserved locomotives which are currently passed for operation on the National Railway network are included. Others, which may still be Network Rail registered but not at present certified for use, are not included, but can be found in the Platform 5 book, "Preserved Locomotives of British Railways".

LAYOUT OF INFORMATION

Locomotive classes are listed in numerical order of class. Principal details and dimensions are quoted for each class in metric and/or imperial units as considered appropriate bearing in mind common UK usage.

The heading "Total" indicates how many of that particular class are listed in this book.

Where numbers actually carried are different from those officially allocated, these are noted in class headings where appropriate. Where locomotives have been recently renumbered, the most immediate previous number is shown in parentheses. Each entry is laid out as in the following example:

No.	Detail	Livery	Owner	Pool	Allocn.	Name
60055 +		**DC**	DC	DCRS	TO	Thomas Barnado

Detail Differences. Only detail differences which currently affect the areas and types of train which locomotives may work are shown. Where such differences occur within a class or part class, they are shown in the "Detail" column alongside the individual locomotive number.

Codes: Codes are used to denote the livery, owner, pool and depot of each locomotive. Details of these will be found in section 6 of this book.

The owner is the responsible custodian of the locomotive and this may not always be the legal owner. Actual ownership can be very complicated. Some vehicles are owned by finance/leasing companies. Others are owned by subsidiary companies of a holding company or by an associate company of the responsible custodian or operator.

Depot allocation codes for all locomotives are shown in this book (apart from shunting locomotives where the actual location of each is shown). It should be noted that today much locomotive maintenance is undertaken away from these depots. This may be undertaken at fuelling points, berthing sidings or similar, or by mobile maintenance teams. Therefore locomotives in particular may not return to their "home" depots as often as in the past.

(S) denotes that the locomotive is stored (the actual location is shown).

Names: Only names carried with official sanction are listed. Names are shown in UPPER/lower case characters as actually shown on the name carried on the locomotive.

GENERAL INFORMATION

CLASSIFICATION AND NUMBERING

All locomotives are classified and allocated numbers under the TOPS numbering system, introduced in 1972. This comprises a two-digit class number followed by a three-digit serial number.

For diesel locomotives, class numbers offer an indication of engine horsepower as shown in the table below.

Class No. Range	Engine hp
01–14	0–799
15–20	800–1000
21–31	1001–1499
32–39	1500–1999
40–54, 57	2000–2999
55–56, 58–70	3000+

For electric locomotives class numbers are allocated in ascending numerical order under the following scheme:

Class 71–80   Direct current and DC/diesel dual system locomotives.
Class 81 onwards   Alternating current and AC/DC dual system locomotives.

Numbers in the 89101–89999 series are allocated to locomotives which have been deregistered but subsequently re-registered for use on the national railway network and whose original number has already been reused. These numbers are normally only carried inside locomotive cabs and are not carried externally in normal circumstances.

WHEEL ARRANGEMENT

For main line locomotives the number of driven axles on a bogie or frame is denoted by a letter (A = 1, B = 2, C = 3 etc) and the number of non-powered axles is denoted by a number. The use of the letter "o" after a letter indicates each axle is individually powered, whilst the "+" symbol indicates bogies are inter-coupled.

For shunting locomotives, the Whyte notation is used. In this notation the number of leading wheels are given, followed by the number of driving wheels and then the trailing wheels.

UNITS OF MEASUREMENT

All dimensions and weights are quoted for locomotives in an "as new" condition with all necessary supplies (eg oil, water and sand) on board. Dimensions are quoted in the order length x width. Lengths quoted are over buffers or couplers as appropriate. All widths quoted are maxima. Where two different wheel diameter dimensions are shown, the first refers to powered wheels and the second refers to non-powered wheels. All weights are shown as metric tonnes (t = tonnes).

HAULAGE CAPABILITY OF DIESEL LOCOMOTIVES

The haulage capability of a diesel locomotive depends upon three basic factors:

1. Adhesive weight. The greater the weight on the driving wheels, the greater the adhesion and more tractive power can be applied before wheelslip occurs.

2. The characteristics of its transmission. To start a train the locomotive has to exert a pull at standstill. A direct drive diesel engine cannot do this, hence the need for transmission. This may be mechanical, hydraulic or electric. The present British Standard for locomotives is electric transmission. Here the diesel engine drives a generator or alternator and the current produced is fed to the traction motors. The force produced by each driven wheel depends on the current in its traction motor. In other words, the larger the current, the harder it pulls. As the locomotive speed increases, the current in the traction motor falls, hence the *Maximum Tractive Effort* is the maximum force at its wheels the locomotive can exert at a standstill. The electrical equipment cannot take such high currents for long without overheating. Hence the *Continuous Tractive Effort* is quoted which represents the current which the equipment can take continuously.

3. The power of its engine. Not all power reaches the rail, as electrical machines are approximately 90% efficient. As the electrical energy passes through two such machines (the generator or alternator and the traction motors), the *Power at Rail* is approximately 81% (90% of 90%) of the engine power, less a further amount used for auxiliary equipment such as radiator fans, traction motor blowers, air compressors, battery charging, cab heating, Electric Train Supply (ETS) etc. The power of the locomotive is proportional to the tractive effort times the speed. Hence when on full power there is a speed corresponding to the continuous tractive effort.

HAULAGE CAPABILITY OF ELECTRIC LOCOMOTIVES

Unlike a diesel locomotive, an electric locomotive does not develop its power on board and its performance is determined only by two factors, namely its weight and the characteristics of its electrical equipment. Whereas a diesel locomotive tends to be a constant power machine, the power of an electric locomotive varies considerably. Up to a certain speed it can produce virtually a constant tractive effort. Hence power rises with speed according to the formula given in section three above, until a maximum speed is reached at which tractive effort falls, such that the power also falls. Hence the power at the speed corresponding to the maximum tractive effort is lower than the maximum speed.

BRAKE FORCE

Brake Force (also known as brake power) is a measure of the braking power of a locomotive. The Brake Force available is dependant on the adhesion between the rail and the wheels being braked and the normal reaction of the rail on the wheels being braked (and hence on the weight per braked wheel). A locomotive's Brake Force is shown on its data panels so operating staff can ensure sufficient brake power is available for specific trains.

ELECTRIC TRAIN SUPPLY (ETS)

A number of locomotives are equipped to provide a supply of electricity to the train being hauled to power auxiliaries such as heating, cooling fans, air conditioning and kitchen equipment. ETS is provided from the locomotive by means of a separate alternator (except Class 33 locomotives, which have a DC generator). The ETS index of a locomotive is a measure of the electrical power available for train supply. Class 55 locomotives provide an ETS directly from one of their traction generators into the train supply.

Similarly, most locomotive-hauled carriages also have an ETS index, which in this case is a measure of the power required to operate equipment mounted in the carriage. The sum of the ETS indices of all the hauled vehicles in a train must not exceed the ETS index of the locomotive.

ETS is commonly (but incorrectly) known as ETH (Electric Train Heating), which is a throwback to the days before locomotive-hauled carriages were equipped with electrically powered auxiliary equipment other than for train heating.

ROUTE AVAILABILITY (RA)

This is a measure of a railway vehicle's axle load. The higher the axle load of a vehicle, the higher the RA number on a scale from 1 to 10. Each Network Rail route has a RA number and in general no vehicle with a higher RA number may travel on that route without special clearance.

MULTIPLE WORKING

Multiple working between vehicles (ie two or more powered vehicles being driven from one cab) is facilitated by jumper cables connecting the vehicles. However, not all types of locomotive are compatible with each other, and a number of different systems are in use. Some are compatible with others, some are not. BR used "multiple working codes" to designate which locomotives were compatible. The list below shows which classes of locomotives are compatible with each other – the former BR multiple working code being shown in brackets. It should be noted that some locomotives have had the equipment removed or made inoperable.

With other classes:
Classes 20, 25, 31, 33, 37 40 & 73/1*. (Blue Star)
Classes 56 & 58. (Red Diamond)
Classes 59, 66, 67, 68, 70, 73/9 & 88.
* DRS has since adapted the systems so its Classes 20/3, 37 & 57 can work with each other only.

With other members of same class only:
Class 43, Class 47 (Green Circle), Class 50 (Orange Square), Class 60.

PUSH-PULL OPERATION

Some locomotives are modified to operate passenger and service (formed of laboratory, test and inspection carriages) trains in "push-pull" mode – which allows the train to be driven from either end – either with locomotives at each end (both under power) or with a driving brake van at one end and a locomotive at the other. Various different systems are now in use. Electric locomotive Classes 86, 87, 90 & 91 use a time-division multiplex (TDM) system for push-pull working which utilises the existing Railway Clearing House (RCH) jumper cables fitted to carriages. Previously these cables had only been used to control train lighting and public address systems.

More recently locomotives of Classes 67 and 68 have used the Association of American Railroads (AAR) system.

ABBREVIATIONS

Standard abbreviations used in this section of the book are:

a	Train air brake equipment only.
b	Drophead buckeye couplers.
c	Scharfenberg couplers.
d	Fitted with retractable Dellner couplers.
e	European Railway Traffic Management System (ERTMS) signalling equipment fitted.
k	Fitted with Swinghead Automatic "buckeye" combination couplers.
p	Train air, vacuum and electro-pneumatic brakes.
r	Radio Electric Token Block signalling equipment fitted.
s	Slow Speed Control equipment.
v	Train vacuum brake only.
x	Train air and vacuum brakes ("Dual brakes").
+	Additional fuel tank capacity.
§	Sandite laying equipment.

In all cases use of the above abbreviations indicates the equipment in question is normally operable. The definition of non-standard abbreviations and symbols is detailed in individual class headings.

1.1. DIESEL SHUNTING LOCOMOTIVES

All BR design shunting locomotives still in existence, apart from those considered to be preserved, are listed together in this section. Preserved shunting locomotives are listed in the Platform 5 publication "Preserved Locomotives of British Railways" (a small number are listed in both that book and in this publication).

Few shunting locomotives have engineering acceptance and are equipped to operate on Network Rail infrastructure (beyond interface infrastructure), but those that are known to be permitted are indicated here.

For shunting locomotives, instead of the two-letter depot code, actual locations at the time of publication are given. Pool codes for shunting locomotives are not shown.

CLASS 03   BR/GARDNER   0-6-0

Built: 1958–62 by BR at Swindon or Doncaster Works.
Engine: Gardner 8L3 of 152 kW (204 hp) at 1200 rpm.
Transmission: Mechanical. Fluidrive type 23 hydraulic coupling to Wilson-Drewry CA5R7 gearbox with SCG type RF11 final drive.
Maximum Tractive Effort: 68 kN (15300 lbf).
Continuous Tractive Effort: 68 kN (15300 lbf) at 3.75 mph.
Train Brakes: Air & vacuum.
Brake Force: 13 t.	**Dimensions:** 7.93 x 2.59 m.
Weight: 31.3 t.	**Wheel Diameter:** 1092 mm.
Design Speed: 28.5 mph.	**Maximum Speed:** 28.5 mph.
Fuel Capacity: 1364 litres.	**Route Availability:** 1.
Train Supply: Not equipped.	**Total:** 3.

Number Notes Livery Owner Location

Number	Notes	Livery	Owner	Location
03084		G	WC	West Coast Railway Company, Carnforth Depot
03196	B		WC	West Coast Railway Company, Carnforth Depot
D2381	v	G	WC	West Coast Railway Company, Carnforth Depot

CLASS 07   BR/RUSTON & HORNSBY   0-6-0

Built: 1962 by Ruston & Hornsby, Lincoln.
Engine: Paxman 6RPHL Mk III of 205 kW (275 hp) at 1360 rpm.
Transmission: Electric. One AEI RTB 6652 traction motor.
Maximum Tractive Effort: 126 kN (28240 lbf).
Continuous Tractive Effort: 71 kN (15950 lbf) at 4.38 mph.
Train Brakes: Vacuum.
Brake Force:	**Dimensions:** 8.17 x 2.59 m.
Weight: 43.6 t.	**Wheel Diameter:** 1067 mm.
Design Speed: 20 mph.	**Maximum Speed:** 20 mph.
Fuel Capacity: 1400 litres.	**Train Supply:** Not equipped.
Total: 1.	

Number	Notes	Livery	Owner	Location
07007	v	B	AF	Arlington Fleet Services, Eastleigh Works, Hants

CLASS 08   BR/ENGLISH ELECTRIC   0-6-0

Built: 1955–62 by BR at Crewe, Darlington, Derby Locomotive, Doncaster or Horwich Works.
Engine: English Electric 6KT of 298 kW (400 hp) at 680 rpm.
Main Generator: English Electric 801.
Traction Motors: Two English Electric 506.
Maximum Tractive Effort: 156 kN (35000 lbf).
Continuous Tractive Effort: 49 kN (11100 lbf) at 8.8 mph.
Power at Rail: 194 kW (260 hp).   **Train Brakes:** Air & vacuum.
Brake Force: 19 t.   **Dimensions:** 8.92 x 2.59 m.
Weight: 49.6–50.4 t.   **Wheel Diameter:** 1372 mm.
Design Speed: 20 mph.   **Maximum Speed:** 15 mph.
Fuel Capacity: 3037 litres.   **Route Availability:** 5.
Train Supply: Not equipped.   **Total:** 172.

* Locomotives with engineering acceptance to operate on Network Rail infrastructure. 08850 has acceptance for use between Battersby and Whitby only, for rescue purposes.

† – Fitted with remote control equipment.

Non-standard liveries:

08308	All over ScotRail Caledonian Sleeper purple.
08401	Dark green.
08442	Dark grey lower bodyside & light grey upper bodyside.
08445	Yellow, blue & green.
08447	Lilac.
08502	Mid blue.
08568	Dark grey lower bodyside & light grey upper bodyside. Red solebar stripe.
08598	Yellow.
08600	Red with a light grey roof.
08630	Black with red cabsides and solebar stripe.
08645	All over black with a white cross.
08682	Multi-coloured.
08730	ABP Ports blue
08774	Red with a light grey roof.
08899	Crimson lake.
08956	Serco Railtest green.

Number	Notes	Livery	Owner	Location
08220	v	B	EE	Nottingham Transport Heritage Centre, Ruddington
08308	a	0	RL	Weardale Railway, Wolsingham, County Durham
08331		K	20	Midland Railway-Butterley, Derbyshire
08375	a	RL	RL	Victoria Group, Port of Boston, Boston
08389	at	E	HN	Celsa Steel UK, Tremorfa Steelworks, Cardiff
08401	a	0	ED	Hams Hall Distribution Park, Coleshill, Warwickshire
08405	at	E	RS	East Midlands Railway, Neville Hill Depot, Leeds
08410	* a	GW	AD	AV Dawson, Ayrton Rail Terminal, Middlesbrough
08411	* a	B	RS	RSS, Rye Farm, Wishaw, Sutton Coldfield (S)
08417	* a	Y	NR	Rowsley, Peak Rail, Derbyshire (S)
08418	a	E	WC	West Coast Railway Company, Carnforth Depot

08423	a	**RL**	RL	PD Ports, Teesport, Grangetown, Middlesbrough
08428	ak	**E**	HN	Barrow Hill Roundhouse, Chesterfield, Derbys (S)
08441	* a	**RS**	RS	Greater Anglia, Crown Point Depot, Norwich
08442	a	**0**	AV	Arriva TrainCare, Eastleigh Depot, Hampshire (S)
08445	a	**0**	ED	Daventry International Railfreight Terminal, Crick
08447	a	**0**	RU	Assenta Rail, Hamilton, Glasgow (S)
08451	*	**B**	AM	Alstom, Longsight Depot, Manchester
08454	*	**B**	AM	Alstom, Widnes Technology Centre, Merseyside
08460	a	**RS**	RS	Felixstowe FLT
08472	* a	**WA**	ED	Hitachi, Craigentinny Depot, Edinburgh
08480	* a	**RS**	RS	Felixstowe FLT
08483	* a	**K**	LS	L&NWR Heritage Company, Crewe Diesel Depot
08484	a	**RS**	RS	Greater Anglia, Crown Point Depot, Norwich
08485	a	**B**	WC	West Coast Railway Company, Carnforth Depot
08499	a	**B**	CS	Colas Rail, Canton Depot, Cardiff
08500		**E**	HN	HNRC, Worksop Depot, Nottinghamshire (S)
08502		**0**	HN	East Kent Light Railway, Shepherdswell, Kent (S)
08507	a	**RB**	RV	Arlington Fleet Services, Eastleigh Works
08511	a	**RS**	RS	GB Railfreight, Eastleigh East Yard
08516	a	**LW**	RS	Arriva TrainCare, Bristol Barton Hill Depot
08523	*	**B**	RL	Weardale Railway, Wolsingham, County Durham
08525		**ST**	EM	East Midlands Railway, Neville Hill Depot, Leeds (S)
08527		**FA**	HN	Attero Recycling, Rossington, Doncaster
08530	*	**FL**	FL	LH Group, Barton-under-Needwood, Staffordshire
08531	* a	**FH**	FL	Freightliner, Felixstowe FLT
08536		**B**	RS	RSS, Rye Farm, Wishaw, Sutton Coldfield (S)
08567		**E**	AF	Arlington Fleet Services, Eastleigh Works
08568		**0**	RS	RSS, Rye Farm, Wishaw, Sutton Coldfield (S)
08571	* a	**WA**	ED	Daventry International Railfreight Terminal, Crick
08573		**K**	RL	Weardale Railway, Wolsingham, County Durham
08575		**FL**	FL	Nemesis Rail, Burton-upon-Trent, Staffordshire
08578		**E**	HN	HNRC, Worksop Depot, Nottinghamshire (S)
08580	*	**RS**	RS	Garston Car Terminal, Liverpool
08585	*	**FH**	FL	Freightliner, Southampton Maritime FLT
08588		**RL**	RL	Alstom, Ilford Works, London
08593	*	**B**	RS	RSS, Rye Farm, Wishaw, Sutton Coldfield (S)
08596	* a†	**WA**	ED	Hitachi, Craigentinny Depot, Edinburgh
08598		**0**	AD	AV Dawson, Ayrton Rail Terminal, Middlesbrough
08600	a	**0**	AD	AV Dawson, Ayrton Rail Terminal, Middlesbrough
08602		**B**	HN	HNRC, Worksop Depot, Nottinghamshire (S)
08605	†	**DB**	RV	DB Cargo UK, Knottingley Depot
08611	*	**B**	AM	Alstom, Wembley Depot, London
08613		**RL**	RL	Weardale Railway, Wolsingham, County Durham
08615	*	**HU**	ED	Tata Steel, Shotton Works, Deeside
08616		**LM**	WM	West Midlands Trains, Tyseley Depot, Birmingham
08617	*	**B**	AM	Alstom, Oxley Depot, Wolverhampton
08622		**K**	RL	Hanson Cement, Ketton Cement Works, nr Stamford
08623		**DB**	RV	Breedon, Hope Cement Works, Derbys (S)
08624	*	**FH**	FL	Freightliner, Trafford Park FLT
08629		**KB**	EP	UK Rail Leasing, Leicester Depot
08630	†	**K**	HN	Celsa Steel UK, Tremorfa Steelworks, Cardiff

08631		B	LS	Weardale Railway, Wolsingham, County Durham
08632	†	LR	RS	RSS, Rye Farm, Wishaw, Sutton Coldfield
08641	*	B	GW	Great Western Railway, Laira Depot, Plymouth
08643		B	MR	Aggregate Industries, Merehead Rail Terminal
08644	*	B	GW	Great Western Railway, Laira Depot, Plymouth
08645	*	0	GW	Great Western Railway, Long Rock Depot, Penzance
08648	*	K	RL	ScotRail, Inverness Depot
08649		KB	ME	VLR Innovation Centre, Dudley
08650		B	MR	RSS, Rye Farm, Wishaw, Sutton Coldfield
08652		B	RS	RSS, Rye Farm, Wishaw, Sutton Coldfield (S)
08653		E	HN	Long Marston Rail Innovation Centre, Warks (S)
08663	* a	B	HH	RSS, Rye Farm, Wishaw, Sutton Coldfield
08669	* a	WA	ED	Wabtec Rail, Doncaster Works
08670	* a	RS	RS	GB Railfreight, Bescot Yard
08676		E	HN	East Kent Light Railway, Shepherdswell, Kent (S)
08678	a	WC	WC	West Coast Railway Company, Carnforth Depot
08682		0	HN	Breedon, Hope Cement Works, Derbys (S)
08683	*	RS	RS	GB Railfreight, Eastleigh East Yard
08685		E	HN	East Kent Light Railway, Shepherdswell, Kent (S)
08690		ST	EM	East Midlands Railway, Neville Hill Depot, Leeds
08691	*	FL	FL	Freightliner, Crewe Basford Hall Yard, Cheshire
08696	* a	B	AM	Alstom, Wembley Depot, London
08700		B	RL	Alstom, Ilford Works, London
08701	a	RX	HN	Long Marston Rail Innovation Centre, Warks (S)
08703	a	GB	RS	Willesden Euroterminal Stone Terminal, London
08704		RB	RV	Ecclesbourne Valley Railway, Wirksworth, Derbys
08706	†	E	HN	RSS, Rye Farm, Wishaw, Sutton Coldfield (S)
08709		E	RS	RSS, Rye Farm, Wishaw, Sutton Coldfield (S)
08711	k	RX	HN	Nemesis Rail, Burton-upon-Trent, Staffordshire (S)
08714		E	HN	Breedon, Hope Cement Works, Derbys (S)
08721	*	B	AM	Alstom, Widnes Technology Centre, Merseyside
08724	*	WA	ED	Wabtec Rail, Doncaster Works
08730		0	RS	Hanson Aggregates, Whatley Quarry, near Frome
08735	†	AW	AV	Arriva TrainCare, Eastleigh Depot
08737		G	LS	L&NWR Heritage Company, Crewe Diesel Depot
08738		RS	RS	Felixstowe FLT
08742	†	RX	HN	Barrow HIll Roundhouse, Chesterfield, Derbys (S)
08743		B	SU	SembCorp Utilities UK, Wilton, Middlesbrough
08752	†	RS	RS	Arriva TrainCare, Crewe Depot, Cheshire
08754	*	RL	RL	Gemini Rail Group, Wolverton Works, Milton Keynes
08756		DG	RL	Weardale Railway, Wolsingham, County Durham
08757		RG	PO	Telford Steam Railway, Shropshire
08762		RL	RL	Eastern Rail Services, Great Yarmouth
08764	*	B	AM	Alstom, Polmadie Depot, Glasgow
08765		HN	HN	Barrow Hill Roundhouse, Chesterfield, Derbys (S)
08774	a	0	AD	AV Dawson, Ayrton Rail Terminal, Middlesbrough
08780		G	LS	L&NWR Heritage Company, Crewe Diesel Depot
08782	a†	CU	HN	Barrow Hill Roundhouse, Chesterfield, Derbys (S)
08783		E	EY	European Metal Recycling, Kingsbury, nr Tamworth
08784		DG	PO	EMD, Longport Works, Stoke-on-Trent
08785	* a	FG	FL	Freightliner, Ipswich Yard

08786	a	DG	HN	Barrow Hill Roundhouse, Chesterfield, Derbys (S)
08787		B	MR	Hanson Aggregates, Whatley Quarry, near Frome
08788	*	RL	RL	PD Ports, Teesport, Grangetown, Middlesbrough
08790	*	B	AM	Alstom, Longsight Depot, Manchester
08795		K	LL	Chrysalis Rail, Landore Depot, Swansea
08798		E	HN	Barrow Hill Roundhouse, Chesterfield, Derbys (S)
08799	a	E	HN	Shackerstone, Battlefield Line (S)
08802	†	E	HN	RSS, Rye Farm, Wishaw, Sutton Coldfield (S)
08804	†	E	HN	East Kent Light Railway, Shepherdswell, Kent (S)
08805		FO	WM	West Midlands Trains, Tyseley Depot, Birmingham
08809		RL	RL	Hanson Cement, Ketton Cement Works, nr Stamford
08810	a	LW	AV	Arriva TrainCare, Eastleigh Depot, Hampshire
08818		GB	HN	HNRC, Worksop Depot, Nottinghamshire
08822	*	IC	GW	Great Western Railway, St Philip's Marsh Depot, Bristol
08823	a	HU	ED	Tata Steel, Shotton Works, Deeside
08824	ak	K	HN	Barrow Hill Roundhouse, Chesterfield, Derbys (S)
08834		HN	HN	Northern, Allerton Depot, Liverpool
08836	*	GW	GW	Great Western Railway, Reading Depot
08846		B	RS	GB Railfreight, Whitemoor Yard, March, Cambs
08847	*	CD	RL	PD Ports, Teesport, Grangetown, Middlesbrough
08850	*	B	NY	North Yorkshire Moors Railway, Grosmont Depot
08853	* a	WA	ED	Wabtec Rail, Doncaster Works
08865		E	HN	Alstom, Central Rivers Depot, Barton-under-Needwood
08868		AW	HN	Arriva TrainCare, Crewe Depot, Cheshire
08870		IC	ER	Eastern Rail Services, Yarmouth
08871		CD	RL	Weardale Railway, Wolsingham, County Durham
08872		E	HN	European Metal Recycling, Attercliffe, Sheffield (S)
08874	*	SL	RL	PD Ports, Teesport, Grangetown, Middlesbrough
08877		DG	HN	Celsa Steel UK, Tremorfa Steelworks, Cardiff
08879		E	HN	Breedon, Hope Cement Works, Derbys (S)
08885		B	RL	Weardale Railway, Wolsingham, County Durham
08887	* a	B	AM	Alstom, Polmadie Depot, Glasgow
08891	*	FL	FL	LH Group, Barton-under-Needwood, Staffordshire (S)
08892		DR	HN	HNRC, Worksop Depot, Nottinghamshire
08899		0	EM	East Midlands Railway, Derby Etches Park Depot
08903		B	SU	SembCorp Utilities UK, Wilton, Middlesbrough
08904	d	E	HN	HNRC, Worksop Depot, Nottinghamshire
08905		E	HN	Breedon, Hope Cement Works, Derbys (S)
08908		ST	EM	East Midlands Railway, Neville Hill Depot, Leeds (S)
08912		B	AD	AV Dawson, Ayrton Rail Terminal, Middlesbrough
08913		E	EY	European Metal Recycling, Kingsbury, nr Tamworth
08918		DG	HN	Nemesis Rail, Burton-upon-Trent, Staffordshire (S)
08921		E	RS	RSS, Rye Farm, Wishaw, Sutton Coldfield (S)
08922		DG	PO	Melton Rail Innovation & Development Centre, Old Dalby
08924	†	GB	HN	Celsa Steel UK, Tremorfa Steelworks, Cardiff
08925		G	GB	HNRC, Worksop Depot, Nottinghamshire
08927		G	RS	GB Railfreight, Bescot Yard
08933		B	MR	Hanson Aggregates, Whatley Quarry, near Frome
08934	a	VP	GB	GB Railfreight, Whitemoor Yard, March, Cambs
08936		B	RL	Weardale Railway, Wolsingham, County Durham
08937		G	BD	Dartmoor Railway, Meldon Quarry, nr Okehampton

08939		ECR	RS	DB Cargo UK, Springs Branch Depot, Wigan
08943		HN	HN	Barrow Hill Roundhouse, Chesterfield, Derbys
08947		B	MR	Hanson Aggregates, Whatley Quarry, near Frome
08948	c	EP	EU	Eurostar, Temple Mills Depot, London
08950		ST	EM	East Midlands Railway, Neville Hill Depot, Leeds (S)
08954	*	B	AM	Arlington Fleet Services, Eastleigh Works
08956		O	LO	Barrow Hill Roundhouse, Chesterfield, Derbys (S)

Class 08/9. Reduced height cab. Converted 1985–87 by BR at Landore.

| 08994 | a | E | HN | Nemesis Rail, Burton-upon-Trent, Staffordshire (S) |

Other numbers or names carried:

08308	"23"	08737	D3905
08423	"LOCO 2" / "14"	08743	Bryan Turner
08451	LONGSIGHT TMD	08754	"H041"
08460	SPIRIT OF THE OAK	08757	EAGLE C.U.R.C.
08483	Bungle	08762	"H067"
08484	CAPTAIN NATHANIEL DARELL	08774	ARTHUR VERNON DAWSON
08499	REDLIGHT	08780	Zippy / D3948
08525	DUNCAN BEDFORD	08787	"08296"
08558	St. Rollox	08790	M.A. SMITH
08585	Vicky	08805	Robin Jones
08588	"H047"		40 YEARS SERVICE
08602	"004"	08809	"24"
08605	"WIGAN 2"	08810	RICHARD J. WENHAM
08613	"H064"		EASTLEIGH DEPOT
08615	UNCLE DAI		DECEMBER 1989 – JULY 1999
08616	TYSELEY 100 / 3783	08818	MOLLY / "4"
08617	Steve Purser	08822	Dave Mills
08622	"H028" / "19"	08823	KEVLA
08624	Rambo PAUL RAMSEY	08824	"IEMD 01"
08629	Wolverton	08846	"003"
08630	"CELSA 3"	08847	"LOCO 1"
08641	Pride of Laira	08865	GILLY
08644	Laira Diesel Depot	08871	"H074"
	50 Years 1962–2012	08885	"H042" / "18"
08645	St. Piran	08899	Midland Counties Railway
08649	Bradwell		175 1839–2014
08669	Bob Machin	08903	John W Antill
08678	"555"	08924	"CELSA 2"
08682	Lionheart	08927	D4157
08690	DAVID THIRKILL	08934	D4164
08691	Terri	08937	D4167
08703	Jermaine	08950	DAVID LIGHTFOOT
08735	Geoff Hobbs 42		

CLASS 09   BR/ENGLISH ELECTRIC   0-6-0

Built: 1959–62 by BR at Darlington or Horwich Works.
Engine: English Electric 6KT of 298 kW (400 hp) at 680 rpm.
Main Generator: English Electric 801.
Traction Motors: English Electric 506.
Maximum Tractive Effort: 111 kN (25000 lbf).
Continuous Tractive Effort: 39 kN (8800 lbf) at 11.6 mph.
Power at Rail: 201 kW (269 hp).   **Train Brakes:** Air & vacuum.
Brake Force: 19 t.   **Dimensions:** 8.92 x 2.59 m.
Weight: 49 t.   **Wheel Diameter:** 1372 mm.
Design Speed: 27 mph.   **Maximum Speed:** 27 mph.
Fuel Capacity: 3037 litres.   **Route Availability:** 5.
Train Supply: Not equipped.   **Total:** 10.

Class 09/0. Built as Class 09.

09002	G	GB	HNRC, Worksop Depot, Nottinghamshire
09006	E	HN	Nemesis Rail, Burton-upon-Trent, Staffordshire (S)
09007	G	LN	London Overground, Willesden Depot, London
09009	G	GB	Miles Platting Stone Terminal, Greater Manchester
09014	DG	HN	Nemesis Rail, Burton-upon-Trent, Staffordshire (S)
09022	B	VG	Victoria Group, Port of Boston, Boston
09023	E	EY	European Metal Recycling, Attercliffe, Sheffield (S)

Class 09/1. Converted from Class 08 1992–93 by RFS Industries, Kilnhurst.
110 V electrical equipment.

| 09106 | HN | HN | Celsa Steel UK, Tremorfa Steelworks, Cardiff |

Class 09/2. Converted from Class 08 1992 by RFS Industries, Kilnhurst.
90 V electrical equipment.

| 09201 | DG | HN | Breedon, Hope Cement Works, Derbys (S) |
| 09204 | AW | AV | Arriva TrainCare, Crewe Depot, Cheshire |

Other numbers or names carried:

| 09007 | D3671 |
| 09106 | "6" |

1.2. MAIN LINE DIESEL LOCOMOTIVES

CLASS 19

Experimental locomotive being rebuilt by Artemis Intelligent Power from a Mark 3B Driving Brake Van. Part of a project funded by the Rail Safety & Standards Board (RSSB) to test the viability of combining hydrostatic transmission to reduce engine emissions. Conversion work is taking place at the Bo'ness & Kinneil Railway. Full details awaited.

Built: 1988 by BR Derby Works.
Engine: 2 x JCB diesel engines.
Main Generator:
Traction Motors:
Maximum Tractive Effort:
Continuous Tractive Effort:
Power at Rail:
Brake Force:
Design Speed:
Fuel Capacity:
Train Supply:

Train Brakes:
Dimensions: 18.83 x 2.71 m.
Weight:
Maximum Speed:
Route Availability:
Total: 1.

19001 (82113)   **B**   AV   BO

CLASS 20   ENGLISH ELECTRIC   Bo-Bo

Built: 1957–68 by English Electric at Vulcan Foundry, Newton-le-Willows or by Robert Stephenson & Hawthorns at Darlington.
Engine: English Electric 8SVT Mk II of 746 kW (1000 hp) at 850 rpm.
Main Generator: English Electric 819/3C.
Traction Motors: English Electric 526/5D or 526/8D.
Maximum Tractive Effort: 187 kN (42000 lbf).
Continuous Tractive Effort: 111 kN (25000 lbf) at 11 mph.
Power at Rail: 574 kW (770 hp).
Brake Force: 35 t.
Weight: 73.4–73.5 t.
Design Speed: 75 mph.
Fuel Capacity: 1727 litres.
Train Supply: Not equipped.

Train Brakes: Air & vacuum.
Dimensions: 14.25 x 2.67 m.
Wheel Diameter: 1092 mm.
Maximum Speed: 75 mph.
Route Availability: 5.
Total: 29.

Non-standard liveries/numbering:

20056   Yellow with grey cabsides and red solebar. Carries No. "81".
20066   Dark blue with yellow stripes. Carries No. "82".
20096   Carries original number D8096.
20107   Carries original number D8107.
20110   Carries original number D8110.
20142   LUL Maroon.
20168   White with green cabsides and solebar. Carries No. "2".
20227   LUL Maroon.
20906   White. Carries No. "3".

Class 20/0. Standard Design.

20007	G	EE	MOLO	SK	
20056	O	HN	HNRL	SC (S)	
20066	O	HN	HNRL	HO	
20096	G	LS	LSLO	CL	
20107	G	LS	LSLO	CL	Jocelyn Feilding 1940–2020
20110	G	HN	HNRS	WS (S)	
20118	FO	HN	HNRL	WS	Saltburn-by-the-Sea
20121	HN	HN	HNRL	BH (S)	
20132	FO	HN	HNRL	WS	Barrow Hill Depot
20142	O	20	MOLO	SK	SIR JOHN BETJEMAN
20168	O	HN	HNRL	HO	SIR GEORGE EARLE
20189	B	20	MOLO	SK	
20205	B	2L	MOLO	SK	
20227	O	2L	MOLO	SK	SHERLOCK HOLMES

Class 20/3. Direct Rail Services refurbished locomotives. Details as Class 20/0 except:

Refurbished: 15 locomotives were refurbished 1995–96 by Brush Traction at Loughborough (20301–305) or 1997–98 by RFS(E) at Doncaster (20306–315). Disc indicators or headcode panels removed.
Train Brakes: Air.   **Maximum Speed:** 60 mph (+ 75 mph).
Weight: 73 t (+ 76 t).   **Fuel Capacity:** 2909 (+ 4909) litres.
Brake Force: 35 t (+ 31 t).   **RA:** 5 (+ 6).

20301	(20047) r	DS	DR	XSDP	BH (S)	
20302	(20084) r	DS	DR	XSDP	BO (S)	
20303	(20127) r	DS	DR	XSDP	CR (S)	Max Joule 1958–1999
20304	(20120) r	DS	DR	XSDP	BH (S)	
20305	(20095) r	DS	DR	XSDP	BO (S)	
20308	(20187) r+	DS	DR	XSDP	BH (S)	
20309	(20075) r+	DS	DR	XSDP	BH (S)	
20311	(20102) r+	HN	HN	HNRL	WS	
20312	(20042) r+	DS	DR	XSDP	BH (S)	
20314	(20117) r+	HN	HN	HNRL	WS	

Class 20/9. Harry Needle Railroad Company (former Hunslet-Barclay/DRS) locomotives. Details as Class 20/0 except:

Refurbished: 1989 by Hunslet-Barclay at Kilmarnock.
Train Brakes: Air.   **Fuel Capacity:** 1727 (+ 4727) litres.
RA: 5 (+ 6).

20901	(20101)	GB	HN	HNRL	WS	
20903	(20083) +	DR	HN	HNRS	BU (S)	
20904	(20041)	DR	HN	HNRS	BU (S)	
20905	(20225) +	GB	HN	HNRL	WS	Dave Darwin
20906	(20219)	O	HN	HNRL	HO	

CLASS 25   BR/BEYER PEACOCK/SULZER   Bo-Bo

Built: 1965 by Beyer Peacock at Gorton.
Engine: Sulzer 6LDA28-B of 930 kW (1250 hp) at 750 rpm.
Main Generator: AEI RTB15656.   **Traction Motors:** AEI 253AY.
Maximum Tractive Effort: 200 kN (45000 lbf).
Continuous Tractive Effort: 93 kN (20800 lbf) at 17.1 mph.
Power at Rail: 708 kW (949 hp).   **Train Brakes:** Air & vacuum.
Brake Force: 38 t.   **Dimensions:** 15.39 x 2.73 m.
Weight: 71.5 t.   **Wheel Diameter:** 1143 mm.
Design Speed: 90 mph.   **Maximum Speed:** 60 mph.
Fuel Capacity: 2270 litres.   **Route Availability:** 5.
Train Supply: Not equipped.   **Total:** 1.

Carries original number D7628.

Only certified for use on Network Rail tracks between Whitby and Battersby,
as an extension of North Yorkshire Moors Railway services.

| 25278 | **GG** | NY | MBDL | NY | SYBILLA |

CLASS 31   BRUSH/ENGLISH ELECTRIC   A1A-A1A

Built: 1958–62 by Brush Traction at Loughborough.
Engine: English Electric 12SVT of 1100 kW (1470 hp) at 850 rpm.
Main Generator: Brush TG160-48.   **Traction Motors:** Brush TM73-68.
Maximum Tractive Effort: 160 kN (35900 lbf).
Continuous Tractive Effort: 83 kN (18700 lbf) at 23.5 mph.
Power at Rail: 872 kW (1170 hp).   **Train Brakes:** Air & vacuum.
Brake Force: 49 t.   **Dimensions:** 17.30 x 2.67 m.
Weight: 106.7–111 t.   **Wheel Diameter:** 1092/1003 mm.
Design Speed: 90 mph.   **Maximum Speed:** 90 mph.
Fuel Capacity: 2409 litres.   **Route Availability:** 5.
Train Supply: Not equipped.   **Total:** 2.

Non-standard livery: 31452 All over dark green.

31106	**B**	HH		BQ	
31128	**B**	NS	NRLO	BU	CHARYBDIS
31452	**0**	ER	ERSL	YA	

CLASS 33   BRCW/SULZER   Bo-Bo

Built: 1959–62 by the Birmingham Railway Carriage & Wagon Company at
Smethwick.
Engine: Sulzer 8LDA28 of 1160 kW (1550 hp) at 750 rpm.
Main Generator: Crompton Parkinson CG391B1.
Traction Motors: Crompton Parkinson C171C2.
Maximum Tractive Effort: 200 kN (45000 lbf).
Continuous Tractive Effort: 116 kN (26000 lbf) at 17.5 mph.
Power at Rail: 906 kW (1215 hp).   **Train Brakes:** Air & vacuum.
Brake Force: 35 t.   **Dimensions:** 15.47 x 2.82 (2.64 m 33/2).

Weight: 76–78 t.   **Wheel Diameter:** 1092 mm.
Design Speed: 85 mph.   **Maximum Speed:** 85 mph.
Fuel Capacity: 3410 litres.   **Route Availability:** 6.
Train Supply: Electric, index 48 (750 V DC only).
Total: 5.

Non-standard numbering: 33012 Carries original number D6515.

Class 33/0. Standard Design.

33012	**G**	71	MBDL	SW	Lt Jenny Lewis RN
33025	**WC**	WC	AWCA	CS	
33029	**WC**	WC	AWCA	CS	
33030	**DR**	WC	AWCX	CS (S)	

Class 33/2. Built to former Loading Gauge of Tonbridge–Battle Line.
Equipped with slow speed control.

33207	**WC**	WC	AWCA	CS	Jim Martin

CLASS 37   ENGLISH ELECTRIC   Co-Co

Built: 1960–66 by English Electric at Vulcan Foundry, Newton-le-Willows or
by Robert Stephenson & Hawthorns at Darlington.
Engine: English Electric 12CSVT of 1300 kW (1750 hp) at 850 rpm.
Main Generator: English Electric 822/10G.
Traction Motors: English Electric 538/A.
Maximum Tractive Effort: 247 kN (55500 lbf).
Continuous Tractive Effort: 156 kN (35000 lbf) at 13.6 mph.
Power at Rail: 932 kW (1250 hp).   **Train Brakes:** Air & vacuum.
Brake Force: 50 t.   **Dimensions:** 18.75 x 2.74 m.
Weight: 102.8–108.4 t.   **Wheel Diameter:** 1092 mm.
Design Speed: 90 mph.   **Maximum Speed:** 80 mph.
Fuel Capacity: 4046 (+ 7683) litres. **Route Availability:** 5 (§ 6).
Train Supply: Not equipped.   **Total:** 65.

Non-standard liveries and numbering:

37424 Also carries the number 37558.
37521 Carries original number D6817.
37667 Carries original number D6851.
37688 Two-tone trainload freight grey with Construction decals.
37703 Carries the number 37067.
37905 Also carries original number D6838.

Class 37/0. Standard Design.

37025	**BL**	37	COTS	NM	Inverness TMD
37038	a	**DI**	DR	XHHP	CR (S)
37057		**CS**	CS	COTS	NM	Barbara Arbon
37059	ar+	**DI**	DR	XHNC	KM
37069	ar+	**DI**	DR	XHNC	KM
37099		**CS**	CS	COTS	NM	MERL EVANS 1947–2016
37116	+	**CS**	CS	COTS	NM
37165	a+	**CE**	WC	AWCX	CS (S)

37175 a	**CS**	CS	COTS	NM	
37190	**B**	LS	MBDL	CL	
37207	**B**	EP	EPUK	Dudley	
37218 ar+	**DI**	DR	XHNC	KM	
37219	**CS**	CS	COTS	NM	Jonty Jarvis 8-12-1998 to 18-3-2005
37240	**F**	NB	COFS	NM	
37254	**CS**	CS	COTS	NM	Cardiff Canton
37259 ar	**DS**	DR	XHSS	KM (S)	

Class 37/4. Refurbished with electric train supply equipment. Main generator replaced by alternator. Regeared (CP7) bogies. Details as Class 37/0 except:
Main Alternator: Brush BA1005A.   **Power At Rail:** 935 kW (1254 hp).
Traction Motors: English Electric 538/5A.
Maximum Tractive Effort: 256 kN (57440 lbf).
Continuous Tractive Effort: 184 kN (41250 lbf) at 11.4 mph.
Weight: 107 t.   **Design Speed:** 80 mph.
Fuel Capacity: 7683 litres.
Train Supply: Electric, index 30.

37401 ar	**BL**	DR	XHAC	KM	Mary Queen of Scots
37402 a	**BL**	DR	XHAC	KM	Stephen Middlemore 23.12.1954–8.6.2013
37403	**BL**	SP	RAJV	BO	Isle of Mull
37405 ar	**DS**	DR	XHHP	CR (S)	
37407	**BL**	DR	XHAC	KM	Blackpool Tower
37409 ar	**BL**	DR	XHSS	KM (S)	Lord Hinton
37418	**BL**	SB	COTS	NM	An Comunn Gaidhealach
37419 ar	**IC**	DR	XHAC	KM	Carl Haviland 1954–2012
37421	**CS**	CS	COTS	NM	
37422 ar	**DR**	DR	XHAC	KM	Victorious
37423 ar	**DR**	DR	XHAC	KM	Spirit of the Lakes
37424	**BL**	DR	XHAC	KM	Avro Vulcan XH558
37425 ar	**RR**	DR	XHAC	KM	Sir Robert McAlpine/Concrete Bob

Class 37/5. Refurbished without train supply equipment. Main generator replaced by alternator. Regeared (CP7) bogies. Details as Class 37/4 except:
Power At Rail: 932 kW (1250 hp).
Maximum Tractive Effort: 248 kN (55590 lbf).
Weight: 106.1–110.0 t.
Train Supply: Not equipped.

37510 a	**EX**	EP	GROG	LR	Orion
37516 s	**WC**	WC	AWCA	CS	Loch Laidon
37517 as	**LH**	WC	AWCX	CS (S)	
37518 ar	**WC**	WC	AWCA	CS	Fort William/An Gearasdan
37521	**G**	LS	LSLO	CL	

Class 37/6. Originally refurbished for Nightstar services. Main generator replaced by alternator. UIC jumpers. Details as Class 37/5 except:
Maximum Speed: 90 mph.   **Train Brake:** Air.
Train Supply: Not equipped, but electric through wired.

37601 ad	**EX**	EP	GROG	LR	Perseus
37602 ar	**DS**	DR	XSDP	ZG (S)	

37603 a	**DS**	DR	XSDP	LW (S)	
37604 a	**DS**	DR	XSDP	LW (S)	
37605 ar	**DS**	DR	XSDP	ZA (S)	
37606 a	**DS**	DR	XSDP	CR (S)	
37607 ar	**DR**	HN	COTS	BH	
37608 ard	**EX**	EP	GROG	LR	Andromeda
37609 a	**DI**	DR	XSDP	LW (S)	
37610 ar	**BL**	HN	COTS	BH	
37611 ad	**EX**	EP	GROG	LR	Pegasus
37612 a	**DR**	HN	COTS	BH	

Class 37/5 continued.

37667 ars	**G**	LS	LSLO	CL	
37668 e	**WC**	WC	AWCA	CS	
37669 e	**WC**	WC	AWCA	CS	
37676 a	**WC**	WC	AWCA	CS (S)	Loch Rannoch
37685 a	**WC**	WC	AWCA	CS	Loch Arkaig
37688	**0**	D0	MBDL	CL	Great Rocks

Class 37/7. Refurbished locomotives. Main generator replaced by alternator. Regeared (CP7) bogies. Ballast weights added. Details as Class 37/5 except:
Main Alternator: GEC G564AZ (37800) Brush BA1005A (others).
Maximum Tractive Effort: 276 kN (62000 lbf).
Weight: 120 t.   **Route Availability:** 7.

37703	**DR**	DR	XSDP	BO (S)	
37706	**WC**	WC	AWCA	CS	
37712 a	**WC**	WC	AWCX	CS (S)	
37716	**DI**	DR	XHNC	KM	
37800 d	**EX**	EP	GROG	LR	Cassiopeia
37884 d	**EX**	EP	GROG	LR	Cepheus

Class 37/9. Refurbished locomotives. New power unit. Main generator replaced by alternator. Ballast weights added. Details as Class 37/4 except:
Engine: * Mirrlees 6MB275T of 1340 kW (1800 hp) or † Ruston 6RK270T of 1340 kW (1800 hp) at 900 rpm.
Main Alternator: Brush BA15005A.
Maximum Tractive Effort: 279 kN (62680 lbf).
Weight: 120 t.   **Route Availability:** 7.
Train Supply: Not equipped.

37901 *	**EX**	EP	EPUK	LR	Mirrlees Pioneer
37905 †	**G**	UR	UKRM	LR (S)	
37906 †	**FO**	UR	UKRM	BL (S)	

Class 97/3. Class 37s refurbished for use on the Cambrian Lines which are signalled by ERTMS. Details as Class 37/0.

97301 (37100) e	**Y**	NR	QETS	ZA	
97302 (37170) e	**Y**	NR	QETS	ZA	Ffestiniog & Welsh Highland Railways/Rheilffyrdd Ffestiniog ac Eryri
97303 (37178) e	**Y**	NR	QETS	ZA	
97304 (37217) e	**Y**	NR	QETS	ZA	John Tiley

CLASS 40   ENGLISH ELECTRIC   1Co-Co1

Built: 1961 by English Electric at Vulcan Foundry, Newton-le-Willows.
Engine: English Electric 16SVT Mk2 of 1492 kW (2000 hp) at 850 rpm.
Main Generator: English Electric 822/4C.
Traction Motors: English Electric 526/5D or EE526/7D.
Maximum Tractive Effort: 231 kN (52000 lbf).
Continuous Tractive Effort: 137 kN (30900 lbf) at 18.8 mph.
Power at Rail: 1160 kW (1550 hp).   **Train Brakes:** Air & vacuum.
Brake Force: 51 t.   **Dimensions:** 21.18 x 2.78 m.
Weight: 132 t.   **Wheel Diameter:** 914/1143 mm.
Design Speed: 90 mph.   **Maximum Speed:** 90 mph.
Fuel Capacity: 3250 litres.   **Route Availability:** 6.
Train Supply: Steam heating.   **Total:** 2.

40013 Carries original number D213.
40145 Carries original number 345.

40013	**G**	ST	LSLO	CL	Andania
40145	**B**	40	CFSL	CL	

CLASS 43   BREL/PAXMAN   Bo-Bo

Built: 1975–82 by BREL at Crewe Works.
Engine: MTU 16V4000R41R of 1680kW (2250 hp) at 1500 rpm.
(* Paxman 12VP185 of 1680 kW (2250 hp) at 1500 rpm.)
Main Alternator: Brush BA1001B.
Traction Motors: Brush TMH68–46 or GEC G417AZ (43124–152); frame mounted.
Maximum Tractive Effort: 80 kN (17980 lbf).
Continuous Tractive Effort: 46 kN (10340 lbf) at 64.5 mph.
Power at Rail: 1320 kW (1770 hp).   **Train Brakes:** Air.
Brake Force: 35 t.   **Dimensions:** 17.79 x 2.74 m.
Weight: 70.25–75.0 t.   **Wheel Diameter:** 1020 mm.
Design Speed: 125 mph.   **Maximum Speed:** 125 mph.
Fuel Capacity: 4500 litres.   **Route Availability:** 5.
Train Supply: Three-phase electric.   **Total:** 189.

† Buffer fitted.
§ Modified Great Western Railway power cars that can operate with power
door fitted short sets.

43013, 43014 & 43062 are fitted with measuring apparatus & front-end cameras.

Power cars 43013 and 43321 carry small commemorative plates to celebrate
40 years of the HST, reading "40 YEARS 1976–2016".

Non-standard liveries:

43206 and 43312 Original HST blue & yellow. Carry the numbers 43006 and
                  43112

43238 Red

43003		SI	A	HAPC	HA	
43004	§	GW	A	EFPC	LA	Caerphilly Castle
43005	§	GW	A	EFPC	LA	
43009	§	GW	GW	EFPC	LA	
43010	§	GW	GW	EFPC	LA	
43012		SI	A	HAPC	HA	
43013	†	Y	P	QCAR	ZA	Mark Carne CBE
43014	†	Y	P	QCAR	ZA	The Railway Observer
43015		SI	A	HAPC	HA	
43016	§	GW	A	EFPC	LA	
43017		FB	A	SCEL	EP (S)	
43020		FB	A	EFPC	EP (S)	MTU Power. Passion. Partnership
43021		SI	A	HAPC	HA	
43022	§	GW	GW	EFPC	LA	
43023		FB	A	EFPC	EP (S)	
43024		FB	A	SCEL	EP (S)	
43025		FB	A	SCEL	EP (S)	
43026		SI	A	HAPC	HA	
43027	§	GW	GW	EFPC	LA	
43028		SI	A	HAPC	HA	
43029	§	GW	GW	EFPC	LA	
43030		SI	A	HAPC	ZK (S)	
43031		SI	A	HAPC	HA	
43032		SI	A	HAPC	HA	
43033		SI	A	HAPC	HA	
43034		SI	A	HAPC	HA	
43035		SI	A	HAPC	HA	
43036		SI	A	HAPC	HA	
43037		SI	A	HAPC	HA	
43040	§	GW	A	EFPC	LA	
43041	§	GW	A	EFPC	LA	St Catherine's Castle
43042	§	GW	A	EFPC	LA	Tregenna Castle
43043	*	ST	P	SBXL	LM (S)	
43044	*	IC	125	ICHP	RD	
43045	*	ST	P	SBXL	LM (S)	
43046	*	MP	LS	MBDL	CL	Geoff Drury 1930–1999 Steam Preservation and Computerised Track Recording Pioneer
43047	*	ST	LS	MBDL	CL (S)	
43048	*	ST	125	ICHP	RD	
43049	*	IC	LS	MBDL	CL	Neville Hill
43050	*	ST	P	SBXL	RJ (S)	
43052	*	ST	DA	MBDL	RJ	
43053		FB	P	SBXL	LM (S)	
43054	*	ST	DA	MBDL	RJ	
43055	*	MP	LS	MBDL	CL	
43056		FB	P	EFPC	LA (S)	
43058	*	RC	LS	MBDL	CL	
43059	*	RC	LS	MBDL	CL	
43060	*	ST	P	SBXL	LM (S)	
43061	*	ST	P	SBXL	LM (S)	

43062	Y	P	QCAR	ZA	John Armitt
43063	FB	GW	SBXL	LA (S)	
43064 *	ST	P	SBXL	LM (S)	
43066 *	ST	DA	MBDL	RJ	
43069	FB	P	EFPC	LA (S)	
43070	FB	P	SBXL	LM (S)	
43071	FB	P	SBXL	LM (S)	
43073 *	ST	P	SBXL	LM (S)	
43075 *	ST	P	SBXL	LM (S)	
43076 *	ST	DA	MBDL	RJ	
43078	FB	P	EFPC	LA (S)	
43079	FB	P	SBXL	LM (S)	
43082 *	ST	P	SBXL	LM (S)	
43083 *	ST	LS	SBXL	ZG (S)	
43086	FB	P	EFPC	LA (S)	
43087	FB	P	EFPC	LA (S)	
43088 §	GW	FG	EFPC	LA	
43089 *	ST	125	ICHP	RD	
43091	FB	GW	SBXL	LA (S)	
43092 §	GW	FG	EFPC	LA	Cromwell's Castle
43093 §	GW	FG	EFPC	LA	Old Oak Common HST Depot 1976–2018
43094 §	GW	FG	EFPC	LA	St Mawes Castle
43097 §	GW	FG	EFPC	LA	Castle Drogo
43098 §	GW	FG	EFPC	LA	Walton Castle
43122 §	GW	FG	EFPC	LA	Dunster Castle
43124	SI	A	HAPC	HA	
43125	SI	A	HAPC	HA	
43126	SI	A	HAPC	HA	
43127	SI	A	HAPC	HA	
43128	SI	A	HAPC	HA	
43129	SI	A	HAPC	HA	
43130	SI	A	HAPC	HA	
43131	SI	A	HAPC	HA	
43132	SI	A	HAPC	HA	
43133	SI	A	HAPC	HA	
43134	SI	A	HAPC	HA	Gordon Aikman BEM MND Campaigner 1985–2017
43135	SI	A	HAPC	HA	
43136	SI	A	HAPC	HA	
43137	SI	A	HAPC	HA	
43138	SI	A	HAPC	HA	
43139	SI	A	HAPC	HA	
43141	SI	A	HAPC	HA	
43142	SI	A	HAPC	HA	
43143	SI	A	HAPC	HA	
43144	SI	A	HAPC	HA	
43145	SI	A	HAPC	HA	
43146	SI	A	HAPC	HA	
43147	SI	A	HAPC	HA	
43148	SI	A	HAPC	HA	

43149	SI	A	HAPC	HA	
43150	SI	A	HAPC	HA	
43151	SI	A	HAPC	HA	
43152	SI	A	HAPC	HA	
43153 §	GW	FG	EFPC	LA	Chûn Castle
43154 §	GW	FG	EFPC	LA	Compton Castle
43155 §	GW	FG	EFPC	LA	Rougemont Castle
43156 §	GW	FG	EFPC	LA	
43158 §	GW	FG	EFPC	LA	Kingswear Castle
43159	FB	125	ICHP	RD	
43160 §	GW	FG	EFPC	LA	
43161	FB	GW	SBXL	LA (S)	
43162 §	GW	FG	EFPC	LA	
43163	SI	A	HAPC	HA	
43164	SI	A	HAPC	HA	
43165	FB	A	SCEL	EP (S)	
43168	SI	A	HAPC	HA	
43169	SI	A	HAPC	HA	
43170 §	GW	A	EFPC	LA	Chepstow Castle
43171	GW	GW	EFPC	LA	
43172	GW	GW	EFPC	LA	
43174	FB	A	SCEL	EP (S)	
43175	SI	A	HAPC	HA	
43176	SI	A	HAPC	HA	
43177	SI	A	HAPC	HA	
43179	SI	A	HAPC	HA	
43180	FB	GW	EFPC	LA (S)	
43181	SI	A	HAPC	HA	
43182	SI	A	HAPC	HA	
43183	SI	A	HAPC	HA	
43185	IC	A	SCEL	ZK (S)	
43186 §	GW	A	EFPC	LA	Taunton Castle
43187 §	GW	A	EFPC	LA	
43188 §	GW	A	EFPC	LA	Newport Castle
43189 §	GW	A	EFPC	LA	Launceston Castle
43190	FB	A	SCEL	EP (S)	
43191	FB	A	EFPC	EP (S)	
43192 §	GW	A	EFPC	LA	Trematon Castle
43193	FB	P	EFPC	LA (S)	
43194 §	GW	FG	EFPC	LA	Okehampton Castle
43195	FB	GW	EFPC	LA (S)	
43196	FB	P	EFPC	LA (S)	
43197	FB	P	EFPC	LA (S)	
43198 §	GW	FG	EFPC	LA	Driver Stan Martin 25 June 1950 – 6 November 2004/Driver Brian Cooper 15 June 1947 – 5 October 1999

Class 43/2. Rebuilt CrossCountry and former LNER, East Midlands Railway or Grand Central power cars. Power cars were renumbered by adding 200 to their original number or 400 to their original number (former Grand Central), except 43123 which became 43423.

43206 (43006)	**0**	A	IECP	EP (S)
43207 (43007)	**XC**	A	EHPC	LA
43208 (43008)	**XC**	A	EHPC	LA
43238 (43038)	**0**	A	IECP	EP (S)
43239 (43039)	**XC**	A	EHPC	LA
43251 (43051)	**VE**	P	COTS	ZA
43257 (43057)	**VE**	P	COTS	ZA
43272 (43072)	**VE**	P	COTS	ZA
43274 (43074)	**ER**	P	COTS	ZA
43277 (43077)	**VE**	P	COTS	KR (S)
43285 (43085)	**XC**	P	EHPC	LA
43290 (43090)	**VE**	P	COTS	ZA
43295 (43095)	**VE**	A	SCEL	EP (S)
43296 (43096)	**VE**	RA	HHPC	WN (S)
43299 (43099)	**VE**	P	COTS	ZA
43300 (43100)	**VE**	P	IECP	NL (S)
43301 (43101)	**XC**	P	EHPC	LA
43303 (43103)	**XC**	P	EHPC	LA
43304 (43104)	**XC**	A	EHPC	LA
43305 (43105)	**VE**	A	SCEL	EP (S)
43306 (43106)	**VE**	A	SCEL	EP (S)
43307 (43107)	**VE**	A	SCEL	EP (S)
43308 (43108)	**VE**	RA	HHPC	WN (S)
43309 (43109)	**VE**	A	SCEL	EP (S)
43310 (43110)	**VE**	A	SCEL	EP (S)
43311 (43111)	**VE**	A	IECP	EP (S)
43312 (43112)	**0**	A	IECP	EP (S)
43313 (43113)	**VE**	A	IECP	LA (S)
43314 (43114)	**VE**	A	SCEL	EP (S)
43315 (43115)	**VE**	A	IECP	EP (S)
43316 (43116)	**VE**	A	SCEL	EP (S)
43317 (43117)	**VE**	A	SCEL	EP (S)
43318 (43118)	**VE**	A	SCEL	EP (S)
43319 (43119)	**VE**	A	SCEL	EP (S)
43320 (43120)	**VE**	A	SCEL	EP (S)
43321 (43121)	**XC**	P	EHPC	LA
43357 (43157)	**XC**	P	EHPC	LA
43366 (43166)	**XC**	A	EHPC	LA
43367 (43167)	**VE**	A	IECP	EP (S)
43378 (43178)	**XC**	A	EHPC	LA
43384 (43184)	**XC**	A	EHPC	LA
43423 (43123) †	**EA**	RA	HHPC	WN (S)
43465 (43065) †	**EA**	RA	HHPC	ZG (S)
43467 (43067) †	**EA**	RA	HHPC	WN (S)
43468 (43068) †	**EA**	RA	HHPC	ZG (S)
43480 (43080) †	**RA**	RA	HHPC	WN
43484 (43084) †	**RA**	RA	HHPC	WN

CLASS 47   BR/BRUSH/SULZER   Co-Co

Built: 1963–67 by Brush Traction, at Loughborough or by BR at Crewe Works.
Engine: Sulzer 12LDA28C of 1920 kW (2580 hp) at 750 rpm.
Main Generator: TG160-60 Mk4 or TM172-50 Mk1.
Traction Motors: Brush TM64-68 Mk1 or Mk1A.
Maximum Tractive Effort: 267 kN (60000 lbf).
Continuous Tractive Effort: 133 kN (30000 lbf) at 26 mph.
Power at Rail: 1550 kW (2080 hp).
Brake Force: 61 t.
Weight: 111.5–120.6 t.
Design Speed: 95 mph.
Fuel Capacity: 3273 (+ 5887).
Train Supply: Not equipped.

Train Brakes: Air.
Dimensions: 19.38 x 2.79 m.
Wheel Diameter: 1143 mm.
Maximum Speed: 95 mph.
Route Availability: 6 or 7.
Total: 49.

Class 47s exported for use abroad are listed in section 1.6 of this book.

Non-standard liveries/numbering:

47270   Also carries original number 1971.
47501   Carries original number D1944.
47614   Carries original number 1733.
47739   GBRf dark blue.
47773   Also carries original number D1755.
47798   Royal Train claret with Rail Express Systems markings.
47805   Carries original number D1935.
47810   Carries original number D1924.
47830   Also carries original number D1645.

Recent renumbering:

47593 was renumbered from 47790 in 2019.
47614 was renumbered from 47853 in 2019.

Class 47/0. Standard Design. Built with train air and vacuum brakes.

47194 +	**F**	WC	AWCX	CS (S)
47237 x+	**WC**	WC	AWCA	CS
47245 x+	**WC**	WC	AWCA	CS	V.E. Day 75th Anniversary
47270 +	**B**	WC	AWCA	CS	SWIFT

Class 47/3. Built with train air and vacuum brakes. Details as Class 47/0 except: **Weight:** 113.7 t.

47355 a+	**K**	WC	AWCX	CS (S)
47368	**F**	WC	AWCX	CS (S)

Class 47/4. Electric Train Supply equipment.
Details as Class 47/0 except:

Weight: 120.4–125.1 t.
Train Supply: Electric, index 66.

Fuel Capacity: 3273 (+ 5537) litres.
Route Availability: 7.

47492 x	**RX**	WC	AWCX	CS (S)
47501 x+	**GG**	LS	LSLO	CL	CRAFTSMAN
47526 x	**BL**	WC	AWCX	CS (S)

47580 x	**BL**	47	MBDL	TM	County of Essex
47593	**BL**	LS	LSLO	CL	Galloway Princess
47614 +	**B**	LS	LSLO	CL	

Class 47/7. Previously fitted with an older form of TDM.
Details as Class 47/4 except:

Weight: 118.7 t.   **Fuel Capacity:** 5887 litres.
Maximum Speed: 100 mph.

47703	**FR**	HN	HNRL	ZB	
47712	**IC**	CD	LSLO	CL	
47714	**AR**	HN	HNRL	WS	
47715	**N**	HN	HNRL	WS	

Class 47/7. Former Railnet dedicated locomotives.
Details as Class 47/0 except:

Fuel Capacity: 5887 litres.

47727	**CA**	GB	GBDF	LR	Edinburgh Castle/ Caisteal Dhùn Eideann
47739	**O**	GB	GBDF	LR	
47746 x	**WC**	WC	AWCA	CS	Chris Fudge 29.7.70 – 22.6.10
47749 d	**B**	GB	GBDF	LR	CITY OF TRURO
47760 x	**WC**	WC	AWCA	CS	
47768 x	**RX**	WC	AWCX	CS (S)	
47769	**V**	HN	HNRS	BH (S)	Resolve
47772 x	**WC**	WC	AWCA	CS	Carnforth TMD
47773 x	**GG**	70	MBDL	TM	
47776 x	**RX**	WC	AWCA	CS (S)	
47786 x	**WC**	WC	AWCA	CS	Roy Castle OBE
47787	**WC**	WC	AWCX	CS (S)	

Class 47/4 continued. Route Availability: 6.

47798 x	**O**	NM	MBDL	YK	Prince William
47802 +	**WC**	WC	AWCA	CS	
47804 +	**WC**	WC	AWCA	CS	
47805 +	**GG**	LS	LSLO	CL	Roger Hosking MA 1925–2013
47810 +	**GG**	LS	LSLO	CL	Crewe Diesel Depot
47811 +	**GL**	LS	DHLT	CL (S)	
47812 +	**RO**	WC	AWCA	CS	
47813 +	**RO**	WC	AWCA	CS	
47815 +	**GG**	WC	AWCA	CS	
47816 +	**GL**	LS	DHLT	CL (S)	
47818 +	**DS**	AF	MBDL	ZG (S)	
47826 +	**WC**	WC	AWCA	CS	
47828 +	**IC**	D0	LSLO	CL	
47830 +	**GG**	FL	DFLH	CB	BEECHING'S LEGACY
47832 +	**WC**	WC	AWCA	CS	
47841 +	**IC**	LS	LSLS	Margate (S)	The Institution of Mechanical Engineers
47843 +	**RB**	HN	SROG	LR (S)	
47847 +	**BL**	HN	SROG	LR (S)	

47848 +	**WS** WC AWCA	CS	
47851 +	**WC** WC AWCA	CS	
47854 +	**WC** WC AWCA	CS	Diamond Jubilee

CLASS 50   ENGLISH ELECTRIC   Co-Co

Built: 1967–68 by English Electric at Vulcan Foundry, Newton-le-Willows.
Engine: English Electric 16CVST of 2010 kW (2700 hp) at 850 rpm.
Main Generator: English Electric 840/4B.
Traction Motors: English Electric 538/5A.
Maximum Tractive Effort: 216 kN (48500 lbf).
Continuous Tractive Effort: 147 kN (33000 lbf) at 23.5 mph.
Power at Rail: 1540 kW (2070 hp).   **Train Brakes:** Air & vacuum.
Brake Force: 59 t.   **Dimensions:** 20.88 x 2.78 m.
Weight: 116.9 t.   **Wheel Diameter:** 1092 mm.
Design Speed: 105 mph.   **Maximum Speed:** 90 mph.
Fuel Capacity: 4796 litres.   **Route Availability:** 6.
Train Supply: Electric, index 61.   **Total:** 5.

Non-standard numbering:

50007   Running with the number 50014 on one side.
50050   Also carries original number D400.

50007	**GB**	50	CFOL	KR	Hercules
50008	**HH**	HH HVAC		ZG	Thunderer
50044	**B**	50	CFOL	KR	Exeter
50049	**GB**	50	CFOL	KR	Defiance
50050	**B**	NB COFS		NM	Fearless

CLASS 52   BR/MAYBACH   C-C

Built: 1961–64 by BR at Swindon Works.
Engine: Two Maybach MD655 of 1007 kW (1350 hp) each at 1500 rpm.
Transmission: Hydraulic. Voith L630rV.
Maximum Tractive Effort: 297 kN (66700 lbf).
Continuous Tractive Effort: 201 kN (45200 lbf) at 14.5 mph.
Power at Rail: 1490 kW (2000 hp).   **Train Brakes:** Air & vacuum.
Brake Force: 83 t.   **Dimensions:** 20.70 m x 2.78 m.
Weight: 110 t.   **Wheel Diameter:** 1092 mm.
Design Speed: 90 mph.   **Maximum Speed:** 90 mph.
Fuel Capacity: 3900 litres.   **Route Availability:** 6.
Train Supply: Steam heating.   **Total:** 1.

Never allocated a number in the 1972 number series.

D1015	**B**	DT	MBDL	KR	WESTERN CHAMPION

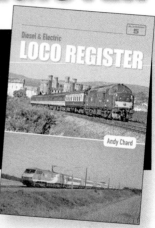

CLASS 55   ENGLISH ELECTRIC   Co-Co

Built: 1961 by English Electric at Vulcan Foundry, Newton-le-Willows.
Engine: Two Napier-Deltic D18-25 of 1230 kW (1650 hp) each at 1500 rpm.
Main Generators: Two English Electric 829/1A.
Traction Motors: English Electric 538/A.
Maximum Tractive Effort: 222 kN (50000 lbf).
Continuous Tractive Effort: 136 kN (30500 lbf) at 32.5 mph.

Power at Rail: 1969 kW (2640 hp).	**Train Brakes:** Air & vacuum.
Brake Force: 51 t.	**Dimensions:** 21.18 x 2.68 m.
Weight: 100 t.	**Wheel Diameter:** 1092 mm.
Design Speed: 105 mph.	**Maximum Speed:** 100 mph.
Fuel Capacity: 3755 litres.	**Route Availability:** 5.
Train Supply: Electric, index 66.	**Total:** 4.

Non-standard numbering:

55002	Carries original number D9002.
55009	Carries original number D9009.
55016	Carries original number D9016.

55002	**GG**	NM	MBDL	YK	THE KING'S OWN YORKSHIRE LIGHT INFANTRY
55009	**B**	DP	MBDL	BH	ALYCIDON
55016	**GG**	LS	MBDL	Margate (S)	GORDON HIGHLANDER
55022	**B**	LS	MBDL	CL	ROYAL SCOTS GREY

CLASS 56   BRUSH/BR/RUSTON   Co-Co

Built: 1976–84 by Electroputere at Craiova, Romania (as sub-contractors for Brush) or BREL at Doncaster or Crewe Works.
Engine: Ruston Paxman 16RK3CT of 2460 kW (3250 hp) at 900 rpm.
Main Alternator: Brush BA1101A.
Traction Motors: Brush TM73-62.
Maximum Tractive Effort: 275 kN (61800 lbf).
Continuous Tractive Effort: 240 kN (53950 lbf) at 16.8 mph.

Power at Rail: 1790 kW (2400 hp).	**Train Brakes:** Air.
Brake Force: 60 t.	**Dimensions:** 19.36 x 2.79 m.
Weight: 126 t.	**Wheel Diameter:** 1143 mm.
Design Speed: 80 mph.	**Maximum Speed:** 80 mph.
Fuel Capacity: 5228 litres.	**Route Availability:** 7.
Train Supply: Not equipped.	**Total:** 29.

All equipped with Slow Speed Control.

Class 56s exported for use abroad are listed in section 5 of this book.

Most of the locomotives at Longport are being rebuilt as Class 69.

Non-standard liveries:

56009 All over blue.
56303 All over dark green.

56007	**B**	GB	UKRS	LT (S)	
56009	**0**	EO	UKRS	LT (S)	
56032	**FER**	GB	GBGS	LT (S)	
56037	**E**	GB	GBGS	LT (S)	
56038	**FER**	GB	UKRS	LT (S)	
56049	**CS**	CS	COFS	NM	Robin of Templecombe 1938–2013
56051	**CS**	CS	COFS	NM	Survival
56060	**FER**	GB	UKRS	LT (S)	
56065	**FER**	GB	UKRS	LT (S)	
56069	**FER**	GB	GBGS	LT (S)	
56077	**LH**	GB	UKRS	LT (S)	
56078	**CS**	CS	COFS	NM	
56081	**FO**	GB	GBGD	LR	
56087	**CS**	BN	COFS	NM	
56090	**CS**	BN	COFS	NM	
56091	**DC**	DC	DCRO	LR	Driver Wayne Gaskell
					The Godfather
56094	**CS**	CS	COFS	NM	
56096	**CS**	BN	COFS	NM	
56098	**FO**	GB	GBGD	LR	
56103	**DC**	DC	DCRO	LR	
56104	**FO**	GB	UKRL	LR (S)	
56105	**CS**	BN	COFS	NM	
56106	**FER**	GB	UKRS	LR (S)	
56113	**CS**	BN	COFS	NM	
56128	**F**	GB		LT (S)	
56301 (56045)	**FA**	56	UKRL	LR	
56302 (56124)	**CS**	CS	COFS	NM	PECO The Railway Modeller
					2016 70 Years
56303 (56125)	**0**	GB	HTLX	LR	
56312 (56003)	**DC**	GB	GBGD	LR	

CLASS 57   BRUSH/GM   Co-Co

Built: 1964–65 by Brush Traction at Loughborough or BR at Crewe Works as Class 47. Rebuilt 1997–2004 by Brush Traction at Loughborough.
Engine: General Motors 12 645 E3 of 1860 kW (2500 hp) at 904 rpm.
Main Alternator: Brush BA1101D (recovered from Class 56).
Traction Motors: Brush TM64-68 Mark 1 or Mark 1A.
Maximum Tractive Effort: 244.5 kN (55000 lbf).
Continuous Tractive Effort: 140 kN (31500 lbf) at ?? mph.
Power at Rail: 1507 kW (2025 hp).   **Train Brakes:** Air.
Brake Force: 80 t.   **Dimensions:** 19.38 x 2.79 m.
Weight: 120.6 t.   **Wheel Diameter:** 1143 mm.
Design Speed: 75 mph.   **Maximum Speed:** 75 mph.
Fuel Capacity: 5550 litres.   **Route Availability:** 6
Train Supply: Not equipped.   **Total:** 33.

Non-standard livery: 57604 Original Great Western Railway green.

Class 57/0. No Train Supply Equipment. Rebuilt 1997–2000.

57001 (47356)	**WC**	WC	AWCA	CS (S)	
57002 (47322)	**DI**	DR	XHCK	KM	RAIL EXPRESS
57003 (47317)	**DI**	DR	XHCK	KM	
57004 (47347)	**DS**	DR	XSDP	LW (S)	
57005 (47350)	**AZ**	WC	AWCX	CS (S)	
57006 (47187)	**WC**	WC	AWCA	CS	
57007 (47332)	**DI**	DR	XHSS	KM (S)	John Scott 12.5.45–22.5.12
57008 (47060)	**DS**	DR	XSDP	LW (S)	
57009 (47079)	**DS**	DR	XSDP	LW (S)	
57010 (47231)	**DI**	DR	XSDP	LW (S)	
57011 (47329)	**DS**	DR	XSDP	LW (S)	
57012 (47204)	**DS**	DR	XSDP	LW (S)	

Class 57/3. Electric Train Supply Equipment. Former Virgin Trains locomotives fitted with retractable Dellner couplers. Rebuilt 2002–04. Details as Class 57/0 except:

Engine: General Motors 12645F3B of 2050 kW (2750 hp) at 954 rpm.
Main Alternator: Brush BA1101F (recovered from Class 56) or Brush BA1101G.
Fuel Capacity: 5887 litres. **Train Supply:** Electric, index 100.
Design Speed: 95 mph. **Maximum Speed:** 95 mph.
Brake Force: 60 t. **Weight:** 117 t.

57301 (47845) d	**DI**	P	GROG	LR	Goliath
57302 (47827) d	**DS**	DR	XSDP	ZG (S)	Chad Varah
57303 (47705) d	**DR**	P	GROG	LR	Pride of Carlisle
57304 (47807) d	**DI**	DR	XHVT	KM	Pride of Cheshire
57305 (47822) d	**RO**	P	GROG	LR	
57306 (47814) d	**DI**	P	XHAC	KM	Her Majesty's Railway Inspectorate 175
57307 (47225) d	**DI**	DR	XHVT	KM	LADY PENELOPE
57308 (47846) d	**DI**	DR	XHVT	KM	Jamie Ferguson
57309 (47806) d	**DI**	DR	XHVT	KM	Pride of Crewe
57310 (47831) d	**DR**	P	GROG	LR	Pride of Cumbria
57311 (47817) d	**DS**	DR	XSDP	ZG (S)	Thunderbird
57312 (47330) d	**RO**	P	GROG	LR	
57313 (47371)	**PC**	WC	AWCA	CS	Scarborough Castle
57314 (47372)	**WC**	WC	AWCA	CS	
57315 (47234)	**WC**	WC	AWCA	CS	
57316 (47290)	**WC**	WC	AWCA	CS	

Class 57/6. Electric Train Supply Equipment. Prototype ETS loco. Rebuilt 2001. Details as Class 57/0 except:

Main Alternator: Brush BA1101E. **Fuel Capacity:** 3273 litres.
Train Supply: Electric, index 95. **Weight:** 113t.
Design Speed: 95 mph. **Maximum Speed:** 95 mph.
Brake Force: 60 t.

57601 (47825)	**PC**	WC	AWCA	CS	Windsor Castle

Class 57/6. Electric Train Supply Equipment. Great Western Railway locomotives. Rebuilt 2004. Details as Class 57/3.

57602	(47337)	**GW** P	EFOO	PZ	Restormel Castle
57603	(47349)	**GW** P	EFOO	PZ	Tintagel Castle
57604	(47209)	**O** P	EFOO	PZ	PENDENNIS CASTLE
57605	(47206)	**GW** P	EFOO	PZ	Totnes Castle

CLASS 58   BREL/RUSTON   Co-Co

Built: 1983–87 by BREL at Doncaster Works.
Engine: Ruston Paxman 12RK3ACT of 2460 kW (3300 hp) at 1000 rpm.
Main Alternator: Brush BA1101B.
Traction Motors: Brush TM73-62.
Maximum Tractive Effort: 275 kN (61800 lbf).
Continuous Tractive Effort: 240 kN (53950 lbf) at 17.4 mph.

Power at Rail: 1780 kW (2387 hp).	**Train Brakes:** Air.
Brake Force: 60 t.	**Dimensions:** 19.13 x 2.72 m.
Weight: 130 t.	**Wheel Diameter:** 1120 mm.
Design Speed: 80 mph.	**Maximum Speed:** 80 mph.
Fuel Capacity: 4214 litres.	**Route Availability:** 7.
Train Supply: Not equipped.	**Total:** 2.

All equipped with Slow Speed Control.

Class 58s exported for use abroad are listed in section 5 of this book.

58012	**F**	PO	BL (S)
58023	**ML**	PO	LR (S)

CLASS 59   GENERAL MOTORS   Co-Co

Built: 1985 (59001–004) or 1989 (59005) by General Motors, La Grange, Illinois, USA or 1990 (59101–104), 1994 (59201) and 1995 (59202–206) by General Motors, London, Ontario, Canada.
Engine: General Motors 16-645E3C two stroke of 2460 kW (3300 hp) at 904 rpm.
Main Alternator: General Motors AR11 MLD-D14A.
Traction Motors: General Motors D77B.
Maximum Tractive Effort: 506 kN (113550 lbf).
Continuous Tractive Effort: 291 kN (65300 lbf) at 14.3 mph.

Power at Rail: 1889 kW (2533 hp).	**Train Brakes:** Air.
Brake Force: 69 t.	**Dimensions:** 21.35 x 2.65 m.
Weight: 121 t.	**Wheel Diameter:** 1067 mm.
Design Speed: 60 (* 75) mph.	**Maximum Speed:** 60 (* 75) mph.
Fuel Capacity: 4546 litres.	**Route Availability:** 7.
Train Supply: Not equipped.	**Total:** 15.

Class 59/0. Owned by Freightliner and GB Railfreight.

59001	**AI**	FL	DFHG	MD	YEOMAN ENDEAVOUR
59002	**AI**	FL	DFHG	MD	ALAN J DAY
59003	**GB**	GB	GBYH	RR	YEOMAN HIGHLANDER
59004	**AI**	FL	DFHG	MD	PAUL A HAMMOND
59005	**AI**	FL	DFHG	MD	KENNETH J PAINTER

Class 59/1. Owned by Freightliner.

59101	**HA**	FL	DFHG	MD	Village of Whatley
59102	**HA**	FL	DFHG	MD	Village of Chantry
59103	**HA**	FL	DFHG	MD	Village of Mells
59104	**HA**	FL	DFHG	MD	Village of Great Elm

Class 59/2. Owned by Freightliner.

59201	*	**DB**	FL	DFHG	MD	
59202	*	**FG**	FL	DFHG	MD	
59203	*	**FG**	FL	DFHG	MD	
59204	*	**FG**	FL	DFHG	MD	
59205	*b	**DB**	FL	DFHG	MD	
59206	*b	**FG**	FL	DFHG	MD	John F. Yeoman Rail Pioneer

CLASS 60   BRUSH/MIRRLEES   Co-Co

Built: 1989–93 by Brush Traction at Loughborough.
Engine: Mirrlees 8MB275T of 2310 kW (3100 hp) at 1000 rpm.
Main Alternator: Brush BA1006A.
Traction Motors: Brush TM2161A.
Maximum Tractive Effort: 500 kN (106500 lbf).
Continuous Tractive Effort: 336 kN (71570 lbf) at 17.4 mph.
Power at Rail: 1800 kW (2415 hp).   **Train Brakes:** Air.
Brake Force: 74 t (+ 62 t).   **Dimensions:** 21.34 x 2.64 m.
Weight: 129 t (+ 131 t).   **Wheel Diameter:** 1118 mm.
Design Speed: 62 mph.   **Maximum Speed:** 60 mph.
Fuel Capacity: 4546 (+ 5225) litres.   **Route Availability:** 8.
Train Supply: Not equipped.   **Total:** 97.

All equipped with Slow Speed Control.

* Refurbished locomotives.

60034 carries its name on one side only.

60500 originally carried the number 60016.

Non-standard and Advertising liveries:

60026   Beacon Rail (blue).
60028   Cappagh (blue).
60066   Powering Drax (silver).
60074   Puma Energy (grey).
60081   Original Great Western Railway green.
60099   Tata Steel (silver).

60001	*	**DB**	DB	WCAT	TO
60002	+*	**GB**	BN	GBTG	TO	GRAHAM FARISH 50TH ANNIVERSARY 1970–2020
60003	+	E	DB	WQCA	TO (S)	FREIGHT TRANSPORT ASSOCIATION
60004	+	E	GB	WQCA	TO (S)
60005	+	E	DB	WQCA	TO (S)
60007	+*	**DB**	DB	WCBT	TO	The Spirit of Tom Kendell
60008		E	GB	WQDA	TO (S)	Sir William McAlpine
60009	+	E	DB	WQDA	TO (S)
60010	+*	**DB**	DB	WCBT	TO
60011		**DB**	DB	WCAT	TO
60012	+	E	DB	WQCA	TO (S)
60013		**EG**	DB	WQDA	TO (S)	Robert Boyle
60014		**EG**	GB	WQCA	TO (S)
60015	+*	**DB**	DB	WCBT	TO
60017	+*	**DB**	DB	WCBT	TO
60018		E	GB	WQCA	TO (S)
60019	*	**DB**	DB	WCAT	TO	Port of Grimsby & Immingham
60020	+*	**DB**	DB	WCBT	TO	The Willows
60021	+*	**GB**	BN	GBTG	TO	PENYGHENT
60022	+	E	DB	WQDA	TO (S)
60023	+	E	DB	WQCA	TO (S)
60024	*	**DB**	DB	WCAT	TO	Clitheroe Castle
60025	+	E	DB	WQCA	TO (S)
60026	+*	**O**	BN	GBTG	TO	HELVELLYN
60027	+	E	DB	WQCA	TO (S)
60028	+	**O**	DC	DCRS	TO
60029		**DC**	DC	DCRS	TO	Ben Nevis
60030	+	E	DB	WQCA	TO (S)
60031		E	DB	WQCA	TO (S)
60032		F	DB	WQCA	TO (S)
60033	+	**CU**	DB	WQCA	TO (S)	Tees Steel Express
60034		**EG**	DB	WQCA	TO (S)	Carnedd Llewelyn
60035		E	DB	WQBA	TO (S)
60036		E	DB	WQCA	TO (S)	GEFCO
60037	+	E	DB	WQCA	TO (S)
60038	+	E	DB	WQDA	TO (S)
60039	*	**DB**	DB	WCAT	TO	Dove Holes
60040	*	**DB**	DB	WCAT	TO	The Territorial Army Centenary
60041	+	E	DB	WQCA	TO (S)
60042		E	DB	WQCA	TO (S)
60043		E	DB	WQCA	TO (S)
60044	*	**DB**	DB	WCAT	TO	Dowlow
60045		E	DB	WQBA	TO (S)	The Permanent Way Institution
60046		**DC**	DC	DCRC	TO	William Wilberforce
60047	*	**CS**	BN	GBTG	TO
60048		E	DB	WQCA	TO (S)
60049		E	DB	WQBA	TO (S)
60051	+	E	DB	WQCA	TO (S)
60052	+	E	DB	WQCA	TO (S)	Glofa Twr – The last deep mine in Wales – Tower Colliery

60053	**E**	DB	WQCA	TO (S)	
60054 +*	**DB**	DB	WCBT	TO	
60055 +	**DC**	DC	DCRS	TO	Thomas Barnardo
60056 +*	**CS**	BN	GBTG	TO	
60057	**EG**	DB	WQDA	TO (S)	
60058 +	**E**	DB	WQCA	TO (S)	
60059 +*	**DB**	DB	WQAA	TO (S)	Swinden Dalesman
60060	**EG**	DC	WQCA	LR (S)	
60061	**F**	DB	WQDA	TO (S)	
60062 *	**DB**	DB	WCAT	TO	Stainless Pioneer
60063 *	**DB**	DB	WQAA	TO (S)	
60064 +	**EG**	DB	WQDA	TO (S)	
60065	**E**	DB	WCAT	TO	Spirit of JAGUAR
60066 *	**AL**	DB	WCAT	TO	
60067	**EG**	DB	WQCA	TO (S)	
60068	**EG**	DB	WQCA	TO (S)	
60069	**E**	DB	WQCA	TO (S)	Slioch
60070 +	**F**	DB	WQDA	TO (S)	
60071 +	**E**	DB	WQBA	TO (S)	Ribblehead Viaduct
60072	**EG**	DB	WQCA	TO (S)	
60073	**EG**	DB	WQCA	TO (S)	
60074 *	**AL**	DB	WCAT	TO	Luke
60075	**E**	DB	WQDA	TO (S)	
60076 *	**CS**	BN	GBTG	TO	Dunbar
60077 +	**EG**	DB	WQCA	TO (S)	
60078	**ML**	DB	WQCA	TO (S)	
60079 *	**DB**	DB	WQBA	TO (S)	
60080 +	**E**	DB	WQDA	TO (S)	
60081 +	**O**	LS	WQDA	TO (S)	
60082	**EG**	DB	WQCA	CE (S)	
60083	**E**	DB	WQCA	TO (S)	
60084	**EG**	DB	WQCA	TO (S)	
60085 *	**CS**	BN	GBTG	TO	
60087 *	**GB**	BN	GBTG	TO	
60088	**F**	DB	WQCA	TO (S)	
60089 +	**E**	DB	WQCA	TO (S)	
60090 +	**EG**	DB	WQDA	TO (S)	Quinag
60091 +*	**DB**	DB	WQAA	TO (S)	Barry Needham
60092 +*	**DB**	DB	WCBT	TO	
60093	**E**	DB	WQCA	TO (S)	
60094	**E**	DB	WQCA	TO (S)	Rugby Flyer
60095 *	**GB**	BN	GBTG	TO	
60096 +*	**CS**	BN	GBTG	TO	
60097 +	**E**	DB	WQCA	TO (S)	
60098 +	**E**	DB	WQDA	TO (S)	
60099	**AL**	DB	WQDA	TO (S)	
60100 *	**DB**	DB	WQAA	TO (S)	Midland Railway - Butterley
60500	**E**	DB	WQCA	TO (S)	

▲ New Freightliner-liveried 08785 is seen at Ipswich on 09/08/21. **Keith Partlow**

▼ In BR green livery, carrying its original number D3948 and the tiny nameplates "Zippy", 08780 is seen shunting outside the Crewe Locomotive Services depot on 04/09/20. **Cliff Beeton**

▲ The veteran Class 20s can still be seen on the main line. On 01/06/21 BR Railfreight grey-liveried 20118 and GBRf-liveried 20901 pass Saxilby running light engine from Worksop to Derby Chaddesden Sidings. **Robert Pritchard**

▼ BR blue-liveried 31128 leads the Branch Line Society's "Sunday Yicker" tour from Ashton-in-Makerfield to Crewe via Liverpool through Roby on 09/06/19.
Steven Harrow

▲ BR Green-liveried 33012 (D6515) arrives at Brockenhurst with a "Swanage Sunday Special" tour from London Waterloo to Swanage hauling the 4TC set on 18/08/19.   **Alan Holding**

▼ New DRS-liveried 37716 passes Leominster with 5V22 08.55 Motherwell–Cardiff Canton movement of Mark 2 stock on 26/08/21.   **Dave Gommersall**

▲ BR Green-liveried D213 (40013) is seen at Crewe with a test working to Telford via Chester on 08/08/18. **Brad Joyce**

▼ ScotRail InterCity-liveried 43127 and 43177 pass Blackford with the 10.33 Aberdeen–Glasgow Queen Street on 21/03/21. **Ian Lothian**

▲ Rail Charter Services-liveried 43059 and 43058 power the 15.09 Skipton–Carlisle "Staycation Express" regular excursion south at Blea Moor, near Ribblehead, on 03/08/21.

Robert Pritchard

▲ InterCity-liveried 47828 heads west with the "Dartmouth Royal Regatta Statesman" tour (the 05.52 High Wycombe–Kingswear) at Stoke Canon on 28/08/21. **Stephen Ginn**

▼ GB Railfreight-liveried 50049 leads 50044 and 50007 into Bescot with the Carlisle–Paddington leg of a 4-day GBRf railtour on 05/09/21. **Dave Gommersall**

▲ Operating a test run on its return to the main line, BR Blue Western D1015 tops GBRf 66719 on 6M42 09.20 Avonmouth–Penyffordd cement at Gossington on 17/09/21. **Dave Gommersall**

▼ Colas Rail-liveried 56105 passes Saxilby with 6C80 08.50 Clarborough Junction–Toton North Yard engineers train on 07/03/21. **Robert Pritchard**

▲ GWR Green-liveried 57603 passes Langham Levels, near Ivybridge, with 5Z79 09.30 Reading–Penzance empty stock move on 05/06/20. **Tony Christie**

▼ Aggregate Industries-liveried 59001 passes Little Bedwyn with 6C76 14.39 Acton Yard–Whatley on 20/07/21. **Tony Christie**

▲ DCR Rail-liveried 60046 is seen near Saxilby with 6Z22 15.21 Leicester Humberstone Road–Worksop empty aggregates on 22/07/21. **Robert Pritchard**

▼ DB Cargo's Puma-liveried 60074 passes Plumley with 6H02 09.30 Warrington Arpley–Tunstead empty stone on 09/06/21. **Cliff Beeton**

▲ DB Cargo-liveried 66175 is seen near Holytown with 4M30 10.30 Grangemouth–Daventry intermodal on 28/08/21. **Stuart Fowler**

▼ New Freightliner-liveried 66623 passes Berkley Marsh with 6V18 Allington–Whatley empty stone on 08/06/21. **Steve Stubbs**

▲ Transport for Wales-liveried 67008 is seen near Leominster with the 17.12 Cardiff Central–Holyhead on 08/06/21. **Dave Gommersall**

▼ New DRS-liveried 68016 and 68001 haul 6M69 15.42 Sizewell–Crewe nuclear flask on Belstead Bank, near Ipswich, on 20/04/21. **Keith Partlow**

▲ BR Revised blue-liveried 69002 (rebuilt from 56311) is shunted by 66776 at the EMD Longport Works on 05/07/21. **Cliff Beeton**

▼ Freightliner-liveried 70001 heads north through Slindon, near Stafford, with 4M61 13.00 Southampton–Trafford Park intermodal on 14/09/20. **Andy Chard**

▲ Colas Rail-liveried 70801 passes Gleneagles with 6A65 05.55 Oxwellmains–Aberdeen cement tanks on 12/04/21. **Ian Lothian**

▼ Caledonian Sleeper-liveried 73971 hauls a single Mark 5 Sleeper coach (15315) along the Angus coast at Boddin, near Usan, running as a 5Z16 15.39 Aberdeen Clayhills–Polmadie on 22/06/21. **Richard Birse**

▲ BR Electric blue-liveried 86259 is seen stabled at Rugby on 24/06/20. **Brad Joyce**

▼ InterCity-liveried 87002 hauls 5Z86 08.45 Crewe–Carlisle empty stock at Red Bank near Warrington on 25/06/20. **Tom McAtee**

▲ New DRS-liveried 88007 approaches Lancaster with 4S44 12.16 Daventry–Mossend intermodal on 04/08/21. **Andy Chard**

▼ New Freightliner-liveried 90014 and 90015 haul a well-loaded 4M80 16.33 Coatbridge–Crewe intermodal south near Abington on 07/07/21. **Stuart Fowler**

▲ One of LNER's remaining Class 91s, 91110 "Battle of Britain Memorial Flight" arrives into Shipley with the 10.25 Bradford Forster Square–London King's Cross on 08/08/21.   **Ian Beardsley**

▼ A rare daytime freight on HS1 on 26/06/20 as two-tone railfreight grey-liveried 92036 leads GBRf 92032 on 6O18 12.40 Ripple Lane–Dollands Moor, 92032 having failed with the booked overnight train.   **Jamie Squibbs**

CLASS 66   GENERAL MOTORS/EMD   Co-Co

Built: 1998–2008 by General Motors/EMD, London, Ontario, Canada (Model JT42CWR (low emission locomotives Model JT42CWRM)) or 2013–16 by EMD/Progress Rail, Muncie, Indiana (66752–779).
Engine: General Motors 12N-710G3B-EC two stroke of 2385 kW (3200 hp) at 904 rpm. 66752–779 GM 12N-710G3B-T2.
Main Alternator: General Motors AR8/CA6.
Traction Motors: General Motors D43TR.
Maximum Tractive Effort: 409 kN (92000 lbf).
Continuous Tractive Effort: 260 kN (58390 lbf) at 15.9 mph.
Power at Rail: 1850 kW (2480 hp).   **Train Brakes:** Air.
Brake Force: 68 t.   **Dimensions:** 21.35 x 2.64 m.
Weight: 127 t.   **Wheel Diameter:** 1120 mm.
Design Speed: 87.5 mph.   **Maximum Speed:** 75 mph.
Fuel Capacity: 6550 litres.   **Route Availability:** 7.
Train Supply: Not equipped.   **Total:** 402.

All equipped with Slow Speed Control.

Class 66s previously used in the UK but now in use abroad are listed in section 5 of this book. Some of the DBC 66s moved to France return to Great Britain from time to time for maintenance or operational requirements.

Class 66 delivery dates. The Class 66 design and delivery evolved over an 18-year period, with more than 400 locomotives delivered. For clarity the delivery dates (by year) for each batch of locomotives is as follows:

66001–250	EWS (now DB Cargo). 1998–2000 (some now in use in France or Poland, ten sold to GB Railfreight and five on long-term hire to DRS).
66301–305	Fastline. 2008. Now used by DRS.
66401–410	DRS. 2003. Now in use with GB Railfreight or Colas Rail and renumbered 66733–737 and 66742–746 (66734[1] since scrapped).
66411–420	DRS. 2006. Now leased by Freightliner (66411/412/417 exported to Poland).
66421–430	DRS. 2007
66431–434	DRS. 2008
66501–505	Freightliner. 1999
66506–520	Freightliner. 2000
66521–525	Freightliner. 2000 (66521 since scrapped).
66526–531	Freightliner. 2001
66532–537	Freightliner. 2001
66538–543	Freightliner. 2001
66544–553	Freightliner. 2001
66554	Freightliner. 2002†
66555–566	Freightliner. 2002
66567–574	Freightliner. 2003. 66573–574 now used by Colas Rail and renumbered 66846–847.
66575–577	Freightliner. 2004. Now used by Colas Rail and renumbered 66848–850.
66578–581	Freightliner. 2005. Now used by GBRf and renumbered 66738–741.

66582–594	Freightliner. 2007 (66582/583/584/586 exported to Poland).
66595–599	Freightliner. 2008 (66595 exported to Poland).
66601–606	Freightliner. 2000
66607–612	Freightliner. 2002 (66607/609/611/612 exported to Poland)
66613–618	Freightliner. 2003
66619–622	Freightliner. 2005
66623–625	Freightliner. 2007 (66624/625 exported to Poland).
66701–707	GB Railfreight. 2001
66708–712	GB Railfreight. 2002
66713–717	GB Railfreight. 2003
66718–722	GB Railfreight. 2006
66723–727	GB Railfreight. 2006
66728–732	GB Railfreight. 2008
66734[11]	GB Railfreight. To be imported from mainland Europe. Details awaited.
66747–749	Built in 2008 as 20078968-004/006/007 (DE 6313/15/16) for Crossrail AG in the Netherlands but never used. Sold to GB Railfreight in 2012.
66750–751	Built in 2003 as 20038513-01/04 and have worked in the Netherlands, Germany and Poland. GBRf secured these two locomotives on lease in 2013.
66752–772	GB Railfreight. 2014
66773–779	GB Railfreight. 2016
66780–789	GB Railfreight. 1998–2000. Former DBC locomotives acquired in 2017 that have been renumbered in the GBRf number series.
66790–792	Built in 2002 as 20018352-3/4/5 (T66403–405) for CargoNet, Norway. Sold to Beacon Rail and leased to GBRf from 2019.
66793–799	Second-hand locos being imported from mainland Europe during 2021–21.
66951–952	Freightliner. 2004
66953–957	Freightliner. 2008 (66954 exported to Poland).

Advertising and non-standard liveries:

66004	I am a Climate Hero (green).
66109	PD Ports (dark blue).
66587	Ocean Network Express (pink with white stripes).
66709	MSC – blue with images of a container ship.
66718	London Underground 150, (black).
66720	Day and night (various colours, different on each side).
66721	London Underground 150 (white with tube map images). Also carries the numbers 1933 and 2013.
66723	Also carries the number ZA723.
66731	Thank you NHS (blue with orange cabsides).
66747	Newell & Wright (blue, white & red).
66769	Prostate Cancer UK (black with blue lettering).
66775	Also carries the number F231.
66779	BR dark green.
66780	Cemex (grey, blue & red).
66783	Biffa (red & orange).
66791	Beacon Rail (all-over blue).
66793	Two-tone trainload freight grey with Construction decals.

66794   Two-tone trainload freight grey with Petroleum decals.
66796   It's Cleaner by Rail (green & blue).
66797   Beacon Rail (all-over blue with yellow solebar stripe and large
        yellow circle logo).

Class 66/0. DB Cargo-operated locomotives.

All fitted with Swinghead Automatic "Buckeye" Combination Couplers except 66001 and 66002.

66031, 66091, 66108, 66122 and 66126 are on long-term hire to DRS.

† Fitted with additional lights and drawgear for Lickey banking duties.

t Fitted with tripcocks for working over London Underground tracks between Harrow-on-the-Hill and Amersham.

66001 t	**DB**	DB	WBAE	TO	
66002	**E**	DB	WBAE	TO	
66003	**E**	DB	WBAE	TO	
66004	**AL**	DB	WBAR	TO	
66005	**MT**	DB	WBAE	TO	Maritime Intermodal One
66006	**E**	DB	WBAR	TO	
66007	**E**	DB	WBAR	TO	
66009	**DB**	DB	WBAE	TO	
66010	**E**	DB	WBAI	TO (S)	
66011	**E**	DB	WBAE	TO	
66012	**E**	DB	WBAE	TO	
66013	**E**	DB	WBAE	TO	
66014	**E**	DB	WBAR	TO	
66015	**E**	DB	WBRT	TO	
66017 t	**DB**	DB	WQAB	TO (S)	
66018	**DB**	DB	WBAE	TO	
66019 t	**DB**	DB	WBAR	TO	
66020	**DB**	DB	WBAE	TO	
66021	**DB**	DB	WBAR	TO	
66023	**E**	DB	WBAT	TO	
66024	**E**	DB	WBAE	TO	
66025	**E**	DB	WBAR	TO	
66027	**DB**	DB	WBAE	TO	
66028	**E**	DB	WBAI	TO (S)	
66030	**E**	DB	WBAR	TO	
66031	**DR**	DB	XHIM	KM	
66032	**E**	DB	WBAI	TO (S)	
66034	**DB**	DB	WBAE	TO	
66035	**DB**	DB	WBAE	TO	Resourceful
66037	**E**	DB	WQAB	TO (S)	
66039	**E**	DB	WBAE	TO	
66040	**E**	DB	WBAR	TO	
66041	**DB**	DB	WBAR	TO	
66043	**E**	DB	WQBA	TO (S)	
66044	**DB**	DB	WBAE	TO	
66047	**MT**	DB	WBAE	TO	Maritime Intermodal Two
66050	**E**	DB	WBAE	TO	EWS Energy

66051	**MT**	DB	WBAR	TO	Maritime Intermodal Four
66053	**E**	DB	WBAE	TO	
66054	**E**	DB	WBAR	TO	
66055 †	**DB**	DB	WBLE	TO	Alain Thauvette
66056 †	**E**	DB	WBLE	TO	
66057 †	**E**	DB	WBLE	TO	
66059 †	**E**	DB	WBLE	TO	
66060	**E**	DB	WBAR	TO	
66061	**E**	DB	WBAE	TO	
66063	**E**	DB	WBAE	TO	
66065	**DB**	DB	WBAR	TO	
66066	**DB**	DB	WBAR	TO	Geoff Spencer
66067	**E**	DB	WBAR	TO	
66068	**E**	DB	WBAR	TO	
66069	**E**	DB	WBAR	TO	
66070	**DB**	DB	WBAE	TO	
66073	**E**	DB	WBAI	TO (S)	
66074	**DB**	DB	WBRT	TO	
66075	**E**	DB	WBAE	TO	
66076	**E**	DB	WBAE	TO	
66077	**DB**	DB	WBAR	TO	Benjamin Gimbert G.C.
66078	**DB**	DB	WBAE	TO	
66079	**E**	DB	WBAR	TO	James Nightall G.C.
66080	**E**	DB	WBAE	TO	
66082	**DB**	DB	WBAE	TO	
66083	**E**	DB	WBAR	TO	
66084	**DB**	DB	WBAR	TO	
66085	**DB**	DB	WBAR	TO	
66086	**E**	DB	WBAE	TO	
66087	**E**	DB	WBAE	TO	
66088	**E**	DB	WBAE	TO	
66089	**E**	DB	WBAR	TO	
66090	**MT**	DB	WBAE	TO	Maritime Intermodal Six
66091	**DR**	DB	XHIM	KM	
66092	**E**	DB	WBRT	TO	
66093	**E**	DB	WBAE	TO	
66094	**DB**	DB	WBAE	TO	
66095	**E**	DB	WBAE	TO	
66096	**E**	DB	WBAE	TO	
66097	**DB**	DB	WBAE	TO	
66098	**E**	DB	WBRT	TO	
66099 r	**E**	DB	WBBE	TO	
66100 r	**DB**	DB	WBBE	TO	Armistice 100 1918–2018
66101 r	**DB**	DB	WBBE	TO	
66102 r	**E**	DB	WBBE	TO	
66103 r	**E**	DB	WBBE	TO	
66104 r	**DB**	DB	WBBT	TO	
66105 r	**DB**	DB	WBAR	TO	
66106 r	**E**	DB	WBBE	TO	
66107 r	**DB**	DB	WBBT	TO	
66108 r	**DR**	DB	XHIM	KM	

66109	**AL**	DB	WBAR	TO	Teesport Express
66110 r	**E**	DB	WBBE	TO	
66111 r	**E**	DB	WBRT	TO	
66112 r	**E**	DB	WBBE	TO	
66113 r	**DB**	DB	WBBE	TO	
66114 r	**DB**	DB	WBRT	TO	
66115	**DB**	DB	WBAE	TO	
66116	**E**	DB	WBRT	TO	
66117	**DB**	DB	WBAE	TO	
66118	**DB**	DB	WBAE	TO	
66119	**E**	DB	WBAE	TO	
66120	**E**	DB	WBAE	TO	
66121	**E**	DB	WBRT	TO	
66122	**DR**	DB	XHIM	KM	
66124	**DB**	DB	WBAR	TO	
66125	**E**	DB	WBAE	TO	
66126	**DR**	DB	XHIM	KM	
66127	**E**	DB	WBAT	TO	
66128	**DB**	DB	WBAE	TO	
66129	**E**	DB	WBAR	TO	
66130	**DB**	DB	WBAR	TO	
66131	**DB**	DB	WBAE	TO	
66133	**E**	DB	WBAE	TO	
66134	**DB**	DB	WBAE	TO	
66135	**DB**	DB	WBAE	TO	
66136	**DB**	DB	WBAE	TO	
66137	**DB**	DB	WBAE	TO	
66138	**E**	DB	WQBA	TO (S)	
66139	**E**	DB	WBAE	TO	
66140	**E**	DB	WBAE	TO	
66142	**MT**	DB	WBAR	TO	Maritime Intermodal Three
66143	**E**	DB	WBAE	TO	
66144	**E**	DB	WBAR	TO	
66145	**E**	DB	WQBA	TO (S)	
66147	**E**	DB	WBAE	TO	
66148	**MT**	DB	WBAE	TO	Maritime Intermodal Seven
66149	**DB**	DB	WBAE	TO	
66150	**DB**	DB	WBAE	TO	
66151	**E**	DB	WBRT	TO	
66152	**DB**	DB	WBAE	TO	Derek Holmes Railway Operator
66154	**E**	DB	WBAE	TO	
66155	**E**	DB	WBRT	TO	
66156	**E**	DB	WBAE	TO	
66158	**E**	DB	WBAE	TO	
66160	**E**	DB	WBAR	TO	
66161	**E**	DB	WBAE	TO	
66162	**MT**	DB	WBAR	TO	Maritime Intermodal Five
66164	**E**	DB	WBAE	TO	
66165	**DB**	DB	WBAR	TO	
66167	**DB**	DB	WBAE	TO	
66168	**E**	DB	WBAR	TO	

66169	E	DB	WBAR	TO	
66170	E	DB	WBAE	TO	
66171	E	DB	WBAR	TO	
66172	E	DB	WBAE	TO	PAUL MELLENEY
66174	E	DB	WBRT	TO	
66175	DB	DB	WBAE	TO	Rail Riders Express
66176	E	DB	WBAR	TO	
66177	E	DB	WBAT	TO	
66181	E	DB	WBAR	TO	
66182	DB	DB	WQBA	TO (S)	
66183	E	DB	WBRT	TO	
66185	DB	DB	WBAE	TO	DP WORLD London Gateway
66186	E	DB	WBRT	TO	
66187	E	DB	WBAE	TO	
66188	E	DB	WBAR	TO	
66190	E	DB	WBAI	TO (S)	
66192	DB	DB	WBAR	TO	
66194	E	DB	WBRT	TO	
66197	E	DB	WBAE	TO	
66198	E	DB	WBAR	TO	
66199	E	DB	WBAE	TO	
66200	E	DB	WBAE	TO	
66205	E	DB	WBAI	TO (S)	
66206	DB	DB	WBRT	TO	
66207	E	DB	WBAE	TO	
66221	E	DB	WBAR	TO	
66230	DB	DB	WQBA	TO (S)	

Class 66/3. Former Fastline-operated locomotives now operated by DRS.
Low emission. Details as Class 66/0 except:

Engine: EMD 12N-710G3B-T2 two stroke of 2420 kW (3245 hp) at 904 rpm.
Traction Motors: General Motors D43TRC.
Fuel Capacity: 5150 litres.

66301 r	DR	BN	XHIM	KM	Kingmoor TMD
66302 r	DR	BN	XHIM	KM	Endeavour
66303 r	DR	BN	XHIM	KM	Rail Riders 2020
66304 r	DR	BN	XHIM	KM	
66305 r	DR	BN	XHIM	KM	

Class 66/4. Low emission. Akiem-owned. Details as Class 66/3.

66413	FG	AK	DFIN	LD	Lest We Forget
66414	FH	AK	DFIN	LD	
66415	FG	AK	DFIN	LD	You Are Never Alone
66416	FH	AK	DFIN	LD	
66418	FH	AK	DFIN	LD	PATRIOT – IN MEMORY OF FALLEN RAILWAY EMPLOYEES
66419	FG	AK	DFIN	LD	
66420	FH	AK	DFIN	LD	
66421	DR	AK	XHIM	KM	Gresty Bridge TMD
66422	DR	AK	XHIM	KM	
66423	DR	AK	XHIM	KM	

66424	**DR**	AK	XHIM	KM	
66425	**DR**	AK	XHIM	KM	
66426	**DR**	AK	XHIM	KM	
66427	**DR**	AK	XHIM	KM	
66428	**DR**	AK	XHIM	KM	Carlisle Eden Mind
66429	**DR**	AK	XHIM	KM	
66430	**DR**	AK	XHIM	KM	
66431	**DR**	AK	XHIM	KM	
66432	**DR**	AK	XHIM	KM	
66433	**DR**	AK	XHIM	KM	
66434	**DR**	AK	XHIM	KM	

Class 66/5. Standard design. Freightliner-operated locomotives. Details as Class 66/0.

66501	**FL**	P	DFIM	LD	Japan 2001
66502	**FL**	P	DFIM	LD	Basford Hall Centenary 2001
66503	**FG**	P	DFIM	LD	The RAILWAY MAGAZINE
66504	**FH**	P	DFIM	LD	
66505	**FL**	P	DFIM	LD	
66506	**FL**	E	DFIM	LD	Crewe Regeneration
66507	**FL**	E	DFIM	LD	
66508	**FL**	E	DFIM	LD	
66509	**FL**	E	DFIM	LD	
66510	**FL**	E	DFIM	LD	
66511	**FL**	E	DFIM	LD	
66512	**FL**	E	DFIM	LD	
66513	**FL**	E	DFIM	LD	
66514	**FL**	E	DFIM	LD	
66515	**FL**	E	DFIM	LD	
66516	**FL**	E	DFIM	LD	
66517	**FL**	E	DFIM	LD	
66518	**FL**	E	DFIM	LD	
66519	**FL**	E	DFIM	LD	
66520	**FL**	E	DFIM	LD	
66522	**FL**	E	DFIM	LD	
66523	**FL**	E	DFIM	LD	
66524	**FL**	E	DFIM	LD	
66525	**FL**	E	DFIM	LD	
66526	**FL**	P	DFIM	LD	Driver Steve Dunn (George)
66528	**FH**	P	DFIM	LD	Madge Elliot MBE Borders Railway Opening 2015
66529	**FL**	P	DFIM	LD	
66531	**FL**	P	DFIM	LD	
66532	**FL**	P	DFIM	LD	P&O Nedlloyd Atlas
66533	**FL**	P	DFIM	LD	Hanjin Express/Senator Express
66534	**FL**	P	DFIM	LD	OOCL Express
66536	**FL**	P	DFIM	LD	
66537	**FL**	P	DFIM	LD	
66538	**FL**	E	DFIM	LD	
66539	**FL**	E	DFIM	LD	
66540	**FL**	E	DFIM	LD	Ruby

66541	**FL**	E	DFIM	LD	
66542	**FL**	E	DFIM	LD	
66543	**FL**	E	DFIM	LD	
66544	**FL**	P	DFIM	LD	
66545	**FL**	P	DFIM	LD	
66546	**FL**	P	DFIM	LD	
66547	**FL**	P	DFIM	LD	
66548	**FL**	P	DFIM	LD	
66549	**FL**	P	DFIM	LD	
66550	**FL**	P	DFIM	LD	
66551	**FL**	P	DFIM	LD	
66552	**FL**	P	DFIM	LD	Maltby Raider
66553	**FL**	P	DFIM	LD	
66554	**FL**	E	DFIM	LD	
66555	**FL**	E	DFIM	LD	
66556	**FL**	E	DFIM	LD	
66557	**FL**	E	DFIM	LD	
66558	**FL**	E	DFIM	LD	
66559	**FL**	E	DFIM	LD	
66560	**FL**	E	DFIM	LD	
66561	**FL**	E	DFIM	LD	
66562	**FL**	E	DFIM	LD	
66563	**FL**	E	DFIM	LD	
66564	**FL**	E	DFIM	LD	
66565	**FL**	E	DFIM	LD	
66566	**FL**	E	DFIM	LD	
66567	**FL**	E	DFIM	LD	
66568	**FL**	E	DFIM	LD	
66569	**FL**	E	DFIM	LD	
66570	**FL**	E	DFIM	LD	
66571	**FL**	E	DFIM	LD	
66572	**FL**	E	DFIM	LD	

Class 66/5. Freightliner-operated low emission locomotives. Details as Class 66/3.

66585	**FL**	HX	DFIN	LD	
66587	**AL**	HX	DFIN	LD	AS ONE, WE CAN
66588	**FL**	HX	DFIN	LD	
66589	**FL**	HX	DFIN	LD	
66590	**FL**	HX	DFIN	LD	
66591	**FL**	HX	DFIN	LD	
66592	**FL**	HX	DFIN	LD	Johnson Stevens Agencies
66593	**FL**	HX	DFIN	LD	3MG MERSEY MULTIMODAL GATEWAY
66594	**FL**	HX	DFIN	LD	NYK Spirit of Kyoto
66596	**FL**	BN	DFIN	LD	
66597	**FL**	BN	DFIN	LD	Viridor
66598	**FL**	BN	DFIN	LD	
66599	**FL**	BN	DFIN	LD	

Class 66/6. Freightliner-operated locomotives with modified gear ratios. Details as Class 66/0 except:

Maximum Tractive Effort: 467 kN (105080 lbf).
Continuous Tractive Effort: 296 kN (66630 lbf) at 14.0 mph.
Design Speed: 65 mph.   **Maximum Speed:** 65 mph.

66601	**FL**	P	DFHH	LD	The Hope Valley
66602	**FL**	P	DFHH	LD	
66603	**FL**	P	DFHH	LD	
66604	**FL**	P	DFHH	LD	
66605	**FL**	P	DFHH	LD	
66606	**FL**	P	DFHH	LD	
66607	**FL**	P	DFHH	LD	
66610	**FL**	P	DFHH	LD	
66613	**FL**	E	DFHH	LD	
66614	**FL**	E	DFHH	LD	1916 POPPY 2016
66615	**FL**	E	DFHH	LD	
66616	**FL**	E	DFHH	LD	
66617	**FL**	E	DFHH	LD	
66618	**FL**	E	DFHH	LD	Railways Illustrated Annual Photographic Awards Alan Barnes
66619	**FL**	E	DFHH	LD	Derek W. Johnson MBE
66620	**FL**	E	DFHH	LD	
66621	**FL**	E	DFHH	LD	
66622	**FL**	E	DFHH	LD	

Class 66/6. Freightliner-operated low emission locomotive with modified gear ratios. Details as Class 66/6 except:

Fuel Capacity: 5150 litres.

66623	**FG**	AK	DFHH	LD

Class 66/7. Standard design. GB Railfreight-operated locomotives. Details as Class 66/0 except 66793 and 66794 which are as Class 66/6.

66701	**GB**	E	GBBT	RR	
66702	**GB**	E	GBBT	RR	Blue Lightning
66703	**GB**	E	GBBT	RR	Doncaster PSB 1981–2002
66704	**GB**	E	GBBT	RR	Colchester Power Signalbox
66705	**GB**	E	GBBT	RR	Golden Jubilee
66706	**GB**	E	GBBT	RR	Nene Valley
66707	**GB**	E	GBBT	RR	Sir Sam Fay GREAT CENTRAL RAILWAY
66708	**GB**	E	GBBT	RR	Jayne
66709	**AL**	E	GBBT	RR	Sorrento
66710	**GB**	E	GBBT	RR	Phil Packer BRIT
66711	**Al**	E	GBBT	RR	Sence
66712	**GB**	E	GBBT	RR	Peterborough Power Signalbox
66713	**GB**	E	GBBT	RR	Forest City
66714	**GB**	E	GBBT	RR	Cromer Lifeboat
66715	**GB**	E	GBBT	RR	VALOUR – IN MEMORY OF ALL RAILWAY EMPLOYEES WHO GAVE THEIR LIVES FOR THEIR COUNTRY
66716	**GB**	E	GBBT	RR	LOCOMOTIVE & CARRIAGE INSTITUTION CENTENARY 1911–2011
66717	**GB**	E	GBBT	RR	Good Old Boy

66718–751. GB Railfreight locomotives.

Details as Class 66/0 except 66718–732/747–749 as below:

Engine: EMD 12N-710G3B-T2 two stroke of 2420 kW (3245 hp) at 904 rpm.
Traction Motors: General Motors D43TRC.
Fuel Capacity: 5546 litres (66718–722) or 5150 litres (66723–732/747–749).

66747–749 were originally built for Crossrail AG in the Netherlands.

66750/751 were originally built for mainland Europe in 2003.

66718	**AL**	E	GBLT		RR	Sir Peter Hendy CBE
66719	**GB**	E	GBLT		RR	METRO-LAND
66720	**O**	E	GBLT		RR	
66721	**AL**	E	GBLT		RR	Harry Beck
66722	**GB**	E	GBLT		RR	Sir Edward Watkin
66723	**GB**	E	GBLT		RR	Chinook
66724	**GB**	E	GBLT		RR	Drax Power Station
66725	**GB**	E	GBLT		RR	SUNDERLAND
66726	**GB**	E	GBLT		RR	SHEFFIELD WEDNESDAY
66727	**MT**	E	GBLT		RR	Maritime One
66728	**GB**	P	GBLT		RR	Institution of Railway Operators
66729	**GB**	P	GBLT		RR	DERBY COUNTY
66730	**GB**	P	GBLT		RR	Whitemoor
66731	**AL**	P	GBLT		RR	Capt. Tom Moore A True British Inspiration
66732	**GB**	P	GBLT		RR	GBRf The First Decade 1999–2009 John Smith – MD
66733 (66401) r	**GB**	P	GBFM		RR	Cambridge PSB
66734[11]						
66735 (66403)	**GB**	P	GBBT		RR	PETERBOROUGH UNITED
66736 (66404) r	**GB**	P	GBFM		RR	WOLVERHAMPTON WANDERERS
66737 (66405) r	**GB**	P	GBFM		RR	Lesia
66738 (66578)	**GB**	BN	GBBT		RR	HUDDERSFIELD TOWN
66739 (66579) r	**GB**	BN	GBFM		RR	Bluebell Railway
66740 (66580)	**GB**	BN	GBFM		RR	Sarah
66741 (66581) r	**GB**	BN	GBBT		RR	Swanage Railway
66742 (66406, 66841)	**GB**	BN	GBBT		RR	ABP Port of Immingham Centenary 1912–2012
66743 (66407, 66842) r	**M**	BN	GBFM		RR	
66744 (66408, 66843)	**GB**	BN	GBBT		RR	Crossrail
66745 (66409, 66844)	**GB**	BN	GBRT		RR	Modern Railways The first 50 years
66746 (66410, 66845) r	**M**	BN	GBFM		RR	
66747 (20078968-007)	**AL**	BN	GBEB		RR	Made in Sheffield
66748 (20078968-004)	**GB**	BN	GBEB		RR	West Burton 50
66749 (20078968-006)	**GB**	BN	GBEB		RR	Christopher Hopcroft MBE 60 Years Railway Service
66750 (20038513-01)	**GB**	BN	GBEB		RR	Bristol Panel Signal Box
66751 (20038513-04) c	**GB**	BN	GBEB		RR	Inspiration Delivered Hitachi Rail Europe

66752–779. Low emission. New build locomotives. Details as Class 66/3.

66752	**GB**	GB	GBEL	RR	The Hoosier State
66753	**GB**	GB	GBEL	RR	EMD Roberts Road
66754	**GB**	GB	GBEL	RR	Northampton Saints
66755	**GB**	GB	GBEL	RR	Tony Berkeley OBE
					RFG Chairman 1997–2018
66756	**GB**	GB	GBEL	RR	Royal Corps of Signals
66757	**GB**	GB	GBEL	RR	West Somerset Railway
66758	**GB**	GB	GBEL	RR	The Pavior
66759	**GB**	GB	GBEL	RR	Chippy
66760	**GB**	GB	GBEL	RR	David Gordon Harris
66761	**GB**	GB	GBEL	RR	Wensleydale Railway Association
					25 Years 1990–2015
66762	**GB**	GB	GBEL	RR	
66763	**GB**	GB	GBEL	RR	Severn Valley Railway
66764	**GB**	GB	GBEL	RR	Major Tom Poyntz Engineer &
					Railwayman
66765	**GB**	GB	GBEL	RR	
66766	**GB**	GB	GBEL	RR	
66767	**GB**	GB	GBEL	RR	King's Cross PSB 1971–2021
66768	**GB**	GB	GBEL	RR	
66769	**AL**	GB	GBEL	RR	LMA LEAGUE MANAGERS ASSOCIATION/
					Paul Taylor Our Inspiration
66770	**GB**	GB	GBEL	RR	
66771	**GB**	GB	GBEL	RR	Amanda
66772	**GB**	GB	GBEL	RR	Maria
66773	**GB**	GB	GBNB	RR	Pride of GB Railfreight
66774	**GB**	GB	GBNB	RR	
66775	**GB**	GB	GBNB	RR	HMS Argyll
66776	**GB**	GB	GBNB	RR	Joanne
66777	**GB**	GB	GBNB	RR	Annette
66778	**GB**	GB	GBNB	RR	Cambois Depot 25 Years
66779	**0**	GB	GBEL	RR	EVENING STAR

66780–789. Standard design. Former DB Cargo locomotives acquired by GB Railfreight in 2017. Details as Class 66/0. Fitted with Swinghead Automatic "Buckeye" Combination Couplers.

† Fitted with additional lights and drawgear formerly used for Lickey banking duties.

66780	(66008)		**AL**	GB	GBOB	RR	The Cemex Express
66781	(66016)		**GB**	GB	GBOB	RR	
66782	(66046)		**GB**	GB	GBOB	RR	
66783	(66058)	†	**AL**	GB	GBOB	RR	The Flying Dustman
66784	(66081)		**GB**	GB	GBOB	RR	Keighley & Worth Valley Railway
							50th Anniversary 1968–2018
66785	(66132)		**GB**	GB	GBOB	RR	
66786	(66141)		**GB**	GB	GBOB	RR	
66787	(66184)		**GB**	GB	GBOB	RR	
66788	(66238)		**GB**	GB	GBOB	RR	LOCOMOTION 15
66789	(66250)		**BL**	GB	GBOB	RR	British Rail 1948–1997

66790–799. Locomotives sourced from mainland Europe.

66790	(T66403)	**GB**	BN	GBBT	RR	
66791	(T66404)	**O**	BN	GBBT	RR	Neil Bennett
66792	(T66405)	**GB**	BN	GBBT	RR	
66793	(29004)	**O**	BN	GBHH	RR	
66794	(29005)	**O**	BN	GBEB	RR	Steve Hannam
66795	(561-05)	**GB**	BN	GBEB	RR	Bescot LDC
66796	(561-01)	**AL**	BN	MBDL	LT (S)	The Green Progressor
66797	(513-09)	**O**	BN	GBEB	RR	
66798	(561-03)	**GB**	BN	GBEB	RR	
66799	(6602)	**U**	BN	GBBR	LT (S)	

Class 66/8. Standard design. Colas Rail locomotives. Details as Class 66/0.

66846	(66573)	**CS**	BN	COLO	HJ	
66847	(66574)	**CS**	BN	COLO	HJ	Terry Baker
66848	(66575)	**CS**	BN	COLO	HJ	
66849	(66576)	**CS**	BN	COLO	HJ	Wylam Dilly
66850	(66577)	**CS**	BN	COLO	HJ	David Maidment OBE

Class 66/9. Freightliner locomotives. Low emission "demonstrator" locomotives. Details as Class 66/3. * **Fuel Capacity:** 5905 litres.

66951	*	**FL**	E	DFIN	LD
66952		**FL**	E	DFIN	LD

Class 66/5. Freightliner-operated low emission locomotives. Owing to the 665xx number range being full, subsequent deliveries of 66/5s were numbered from 66953 onwards. Details as Class 66/5 (low emission).

66953	**FL**	BN	DFIN	LD	
66955	**FL**	BN	DFIN	LD	
66956	**FL**	BN	DFIN	LD	
66957	**FL**	BN	DFIN	LD	Stephenson Locomotive Society 1909–2009

CLASS 67   ALSTOM/GENERAL MOTORS   Bo-Bo

Built: 1999–2000 by Alstom at Valencia, Spain, as sub-contractors for General Motors (General Motors model JT42 HW-HS).
Engine: GM 12N-710G3B-EC two stroke of 2385 kW (3200 hp) at 904 rpm.
Main Alternator: General Motors AR9A/HEP7/CA6C.
Traction Motors: General Motors D43FM.
Maximum Tractive Effort: 141 kN (31770 lbf).
Continuous Tractive Effort: 90 kN (20200 lbf) at 46.5 mph.
Power at Rail: 1860 kW.

Brake Force: 78 t.	**Train Brakes:** Air.
Weight: 90 t.	**Dimensions:** 19.74 x 2.72 m.
Design Speed: 125 mph.	**Wheel Diameter:** 965 mm.
Fuel Capacity: 4927 litres.	**Maximum Speed:** 125 mph.
Train Supply: Electric, index 66.	**Route Availability:** 8.
	Total: 30.

All equipped with Slow Speed Control and Swinghead Automatic "Buckeye" Combination Couplers.

The following locomotives have been modified to operate with TfW Mark 4 stock: 67008, 67010, 67013, 67014, 67015, 67017, 67025.

Non-standard liveries:

67026 Diamond Jubilee silver.
67029 All over silver with DB logos.

67001	**AB**	DB	WAAC	CE	
67002	**AB**	DB	WAAC	CE	
67003	**AB**	DB	WQBA	TO (S)	
67004 r	**DB**	DB	WQAB	TO (S)	
67005	**RZ**	DB	WAAC	CE	Queen's Messenger
67006	**RZ**	DB	WAAC	CE	Royal Sovereign
67007 r	**E**	DB	WABC	CE	
67008	**TW**	DB	WAWC	CE	
67009 r	**E**	DB	WQBA	CE (S)	
67010	**DB**	DB	WAWC	CE	
67011 r	**E**	DB	WQBA	CE (S)	
67012	**CM**	DB	WAAC	CE	
67013	**DB**	DB	WAWC	CE	
67014	**TW**	DB	WAWC	CE	
67015	**DB**	DB	WAWC	CE	
67016	**E**	DB	WAAC	CE	
67017	**TW**	DB	WAWC	CE	
67018	**DB**	DB	WQBA	CE (S)	Keith Heller
67019	**E**	DB	WQBA	TO (S)	
67020	**E**	DB	WAAC	CE	
67021	**PC**	DB	WAAC	CE	
67022	**E**	DB	WQBA	CE (S)	
67023	**CS**	BN	COTS	RU	Stella
67024	**PC**	DB	WAAC	CE	
67025	**TW**	DB	WAWC	TO	
67026	**O**	DB	WQBA	CE (S)	Diamond Jubilee
67027	**CS**	BN	COTS	RU	Charlotte
67028	**DB**	DB	WAAC	CE	
67029	**O**	DB	WQAB	CE (S)	Royal Diamond
67030 r	**E**	DB	WQBA	TO (S)	

CLASS 68   VOSSLOH/STADLER   Bo-Bo

New Vossloh/Stadler mixed-traffic locomotives operated by DRS.

Built: 2012–16 by Vossloh/Stadler, Valencia, Spain.
Engine: Caterpillar C175-16 of 2800 kW (3750 hp) at 1740 rpm.
Main Alternator: ABB WGX560.
Traction Motors: 4 x AMXL400 AC frame mounted ABB 4FRA6063.
Maximum Tractive Effort: 317 kN (71260 lbf).
Continuous Tractive Effort: 258 kN (58000 lbf) at 20.5 mph.

Power at Rail:	**Train Brakes:** Air & rheostatic.
Brake Force: 73 t.	**Dimensions:** 20.50 x 2.69 m.
Weight: 85 t.	**Wheel Diameter:** 1100 mm.

Design Speed: 100 mph.   **Maximum Speed:** 100 mph.
Fuel Capacity: 5600 litres.   **Route Availability:** 7.
Train Supply: Electric, index 96.   **Total:** 34.

68008–015 have been modified to operate in push-pull mode on the Chiltern Railways locomotive-hauled sets.

68019–034 have been modified to operate in push-pull mode with the TransPennine Express Mark 5A stock.

68001	**DI**	BN	XHVE	CR	Evolution
68002	**DI**	BN	XHVE	CR	Intrepid
68003	**DI**	BN	XHVE	CR	Astute
68004	**DI**	BN	XHVE	CR	Rapid
68005	**DI**	BN	XHVE	CR	Defiant
68006	**DR**	BN	XHVE	CR	Daring
68007	**DR**	BN	XHVE	CR	Valiant
68008	**DI**	BN	XHCS	CR	Avenger
68009	**DI**	BN	XHCS	CR	Titan
68010	**CM**	BN	XHCE	CR	Oxford Flyer
68011	**CM**	BN	XHCE	CR	
68012	**CM**	BN	XHCE	CR	
68013	**CM**	BN	XHCE	CR	
68014	**CM**	BN	XHCE	CR	
68015	**CM**	BN	XHCE	CR	
68016	**DI**	BN	XHVE	CR	Fearless
68017	**DI**	BN	XHVE	CR	Hornet
68018	**DI**	BN	XHVE	CR	Vigilant
68019	**TP**	BN	TPEX	CR	Brutus
68020	**TP**	BN	TPEX	CR	Reliance
68021	**TP**	BN	TPEX	CR	Tireless
68022	**TP**	BN	TPEX	CR	Resolution
68023	**TP**	BN	TPEX	CR	Achilles
68024	**TP**	BN	TPEX	CR	Centaur
68025	**TP**	BN	TPEX	CR	Superb
68026	**TP**	BN	TPEX	CR	Enterprise
68027	**TP**	BN	TPEX	CR	Splendid
68028	**TP**	BN	TPEX	CR	Lord President
68029	**TP**	BN	TPEX	CR	Courageous
68030	**TP**	BN	TPEX	CR	Black Douglas
68031	**TP**	BN	TPEX	CR	Felix
68032	**TP**	BN	TPEX	CR	Destroyer
68033	**DI**	DR	XHTP	CR	
68034	**DI**	DR	XHTP	CR	

CLASS 69   BRUSH/BR/RUSTON/EMD   Co-Co

These locomotives are heavy rebuilds of Class 56s for GB Railfreight, with new General Motors engines, the same type as used in the Class 66s. The first rebuild were completed and entered service in 2021 and it is planned that a total of 16 locomotives will be rebuilt. Donor locomotives shown for 69004–010 are provisional.

Built: 1976–84 by Electroputere at Craiova, Romania (as sub-contractors for Brush) or BREL at Doncaster or Crewe Works. Rebuilt 2019–22 by ElectroMotive Diesel Services, Longport.
Engine: General Motors 12N-710G3B-T2 two stroke of 2385 kW (3200 hp) at 904 rpm.
Main Traction Alternator: General Motors EMD AR10/CA6.
Traction Motors: Brush TM73-62.
Maximum Tractive Effort: 280 kN (62900 lbf).
Continuous Tractive Effort: 240 kN (54000lbf).

Power at Rail: 2080 kW.	**Train Brakes:** Air.
Brake Force: 60 tonnes.	**Dimensions:** 19.36 x 2.79 m.
Weight: 125 tonnes.	**Wheel Diameter:** 1143 mm.
Design Speed: 80 mph.	**Maximum Speed:** 80 mph.
Fuel Capacity: 5200 litres.	**Route Availability:** 7.
Train Supply: Not equipped.	**Total:** 16.

69001	(56031)	**GB**	PG	GBRG	TN	Mayflower
69002	(56311)	**GB**	PG	GBRG	TN	Bob Tiller CM&EE
69003	(56018)					
69004	(56069)					
69005	(56007)					
69006	(56128)					
69007	(56037)					
69008	(56038)					
69009	(56060)					
69010	(56065)					
69011						
69012						
69013						
69014						
69015						
69016						

CLASS 70   GENERAL ELECTRIC   Co-Co

GE "PowerHaul" locomotives. 70012 was badly damaged whilst being unloaded in 2011 and was returned to Pennsylvania.

70801 (built as 70099) is a Turkish-built demonstrator that arrived in Britain in 2012. Colas Rail leased this locomotive and then in 2013 ordered a further nine locomotives (70802-810) that were delivered in 2014. 70811-817 followed in 2017.

Built: 2009–17 by General Electric, Erie, Pennsylvania, USA or by TÜLOMSAS, Eskişehir, Turkey (70801).
Engine: General Electric PowerHaul P616LDA1 of 2848 kW (3820 hp) at 1500 rpm.
Main Alternator: General Electric GTA series.
Traction Motors: AC-GE 5GEB30.
Maximum Tractive Effort: 544 kN (122000 lbf).
Continuous Tractive Effort: 427 kN (96000 lbf) at 11 mph.

Power at Rail:	**Train Brakes:** Air.

Brake Force: 96.7 t.
Weight: 129 t.
Design Speed: 75 mph.
Fuel Capacity: 6000 litres.
Train Supply: Not equipped.

Dimensions: 21.71 x 2.64 m.
Wheel Diameter: 1066 mm.
Maximum Speed: 75 mph.
Route Availability: 7.
Total: 36.

Class 70/0. Freightliner locomotives.

70001	**FH**	AK	DFGI	LD	PowerHaul
70002	**FH**	AK	DFGI	LD	
70003	**FH**	AK	DFGI	LD	
70004	**FH**	AK	DFGI	LD	The Coal Industry Society
70005	**FH**	AK	DFGI	LD	
70006	**FH**	AK	DFGI	LD	
70007	**FH**	AK	DFGI	LD	
70008	**FH**	AK	DFGI	LD	
70009	**FH**	AK	DHLT	LD (S)	
70010	**FH**	AK	DFGI	LD	
70011	**FH**	AK	DFGI	LD	
70013	**FH**	AK	DHLT	LD (S)	
70014	**FH**	AK	DFGI	LD	
70015	**FH**	AK	DFGI	LD	
70016	**FH**	AK	DFGI	LD	
70017	**FH**	AK	DFGI	LD	
70018	**FH**	AK	DHLT	LD (S)	
70019	**FH**	AK	DFGI	LD	
70020	**FH**	AK	DFGI	LD	

Class 70/8. Colas Rail locomotives.

70801	**CS**	LF	COLO	CF
70802	**CS**	LF	COLO	CF
70803	**CS**	LF	COLO	CF
70804	**CS**	LF	COLO	CF
70805	**CS**	LF	COLO	CF
70806	**CS**	LF	COLO	CF
70807	**CS**	LF	COLO	CF
70808	**CS**	LF	COLO	CF
70809	**CS**	LF	COLO	CF
70810	**CS**	LF	COLO	CF
70811	**CS**	BN	COLO	CF
70812	**CS**	BN	COLO	CF
70813	**CS**	BN	COLO	CF
70814	**CS**	BN	COLO	CF
70815	**CS**	BN	COLO	CF
70816	**CS**	BN	COLO	CF
70817	**CS**	BN	COLO	CF

2. ELECTRO-DIESEL & ELECTRIC LOCOMOTIVES

CLASS 73/1   BR/ENGLISH ELECTRIC   Bo-Bo

Electro-diesel locomotives which can operate either from a DC supply or using power from a diesel engine.

Built: 1965–67 by English Electric Co. at Vulcan Foundry, Newton-le-Willows.
Engine: English Electric 4SRKT of 447 kW (600 hp) at 850 rpm.
Main Generator: English Electric 824/5D.
Electric Supply System: 750 V DC from third rail.
Traction Motors: English Electric 546/1B.
Maximum Tractive Effort (Electric): 179 kN (40000 lbf).
Maximum Tractive Effort (Diesel): 160 kN (36000 lbf).
Continuous Rating (Electric): 1060 kW (1420 hp) giving a tractive effort of 35 kN (7800 lbf) at 68 mph.
Continuous Tractive Effort (Diesel): 60 kN (13600 lbf) at 11.5 mph.
Maximum Rail Power (Electric): 2350 kW (3150 hp) at 42 mph.
Train Brakes: Air, vacuum & electro-pneumatic († Air & electro-pneumatic).
Brake Force: 31 t.   **Dimensions:** 16.36 x 2.64 m.
Weight: 77 t.   **Wheel Diameter:** 1016 mm.
Design Speed: 90 mph.   **Maximum Speed:** 90 mph.
Fuel Capacity: 1409 litres.   **Route Availability:** 6.
Train Supply: Electric, index 66 (on electric power only). **Total:** 30.

Formerly numbered E6007–E6020/E6022–E6026/E6028–E6049 (not in order).

Locomotives numbered in the 732xx series are classed as 73/2 and were originally dedicated to Gatwick Express services.

There have been two separate Class 73 rebuild projects. For GBRf 11 locomotives were rebuilt at Brush, Loughborough with a 1600 hp MTU engine (renumbered 73961–971). For Network Rail 73104/211 were rebuilt at RVEL Derby (now LORAM) with 2 x QSK19 750 hp engines (73951/952).

Non-standard liveries and numbering:

73110	Carries original number E6016.
73128	Two-tone grey.
73139	Light blue & light grey.
73235	Plain dark blue.

73101	**PC**	GB	GBZZ	ZG	(S)	
73107	**GB**	GB	GBED	SE		Tracy
73109	**GB**	GB	GBED	SE		Battle of Britain 80th Anniversary
73110	**B**	GB	GBBR	ZG	(S)	
73119	**GB**	GB	GBED	SE		Borough of Eastleigh
73128	**GB**	GB	GBED	SE		O.V.S. BULLEID C.B.E.
73133	**TT**	TT	MBED	ZG		
73134	**IC**	GB	GBZZ	LB	(S)	Woking Homes 1885–1985

73136	**GB**	GB	GBED	SE	Mhairi
73138	**Y**	NR	QADD	RO (S)	
73139	**0**		GBZZ	ZG (S)	
73141	**GB**	GB	GBED	SE	Charlotte
73201 †	**B**	GB	GBED	SE	Broadlands
73202 †	**SN**	P	MBED	SL	Graham Stenning
73212 †	**GB**	GB	GBED	SE	Fiona
73213 †	**GB**	GB	GBED	SE	Rhodalyn
73235 †	**0**	P	HYWD	BM	

CLASS 73/9 (RVEL)   BR/RVEL   Bo-Bo

The 7395x number series was used for rebuilt Network Rail locomotives.

Rebuilt: Re-engineered by RVEL Derby 2013–15.
Engine: 2 x QSK19 of 560 kW (750 hp) at 1800 rpm (total 1120 kw (1500 hp)).
Main Alternator: 2 x Marathon Magnaplus.
Electric Supply System: 750 V DC from third rail.
Traction Motors: English Electric 546/1B.
Maximum Tractive Effort (Electric): 179 kN (40000 lbf).
Maximum Tractive Effort (Diesel): 179 kN (40000 lbf).
Continuous Rating (Electric): 1060 kW (1420 hp) giving a tractive effort of 35 kN (7800 lbf) at 68 mph.
Continuous Tractive Effort (Diesel): 990 kW (1328 hp) giving a tractive effort of 33 kN (7420 lbf) at 68 mph.
Maximum Rail Power (Electric): 2350 kW (3150 hp) at 42 mph.
Train Brakes: Air.   **Brake Force:** 31 t.
Weight: 77 t.   **Dimensions:** 16.36 x 2.64 m.
Maximum Speed: 90 mph.   **Wheel Diameter:** 1016 mm.
Fuel Capacity: 2260 litres.   **Route Availability:** 6.
Train Supply: Not equipped.

73951 (73104)	**Y**	LO	QADD	ZA	Malcolm Brinded
73952 (73211)	**Y**	LO	QADD	ZA	Janis Kong

CLASS 73/9 (GBRf)   BR/BRUSH   Bo-Bo

GBRf Class 73s rebuilt at Brush Loughborough. 73961–965 are normally used on Network Rail contracts and 73966–971 are used by Caledonian Sleeper.

Rebuilt: Re-engineered by Brush, Loughborough 2014–16.
Engine: MTU 8V4000 R43L of 1195 kW (1600 hp) at 1800 rpm.
Main Alternator: Lechmotoren SDV 87.53-12.
Electric Supply System: 750 V DC from third rail (73961–965 only).
Traction Motors: English Electric 546/1B.
Maximum Tractive Effort (Electric): 179 kN (40000 lbf).
Maximum Tractive Effort (Diesel): 179 kN (40000 lbf).
Continuous Rating (Electric): 1060 kW (1420 hp) giving a tractive effort of 35 kN (7800 lbf) at 68 mph.
Continuous Tractive Effort (Diesel):

Maximum Rail Power (Electric): 2350 kW (3150 hp) at 42 mph.
Train Brakes: Air.   **Brake Force:** 31 t.
Weight: 77 t.   **Dimensions:** 16.36 x 2.64 m.
Maximum Speed: 90 mph.   **Wheel Diameter:** 1016 mm.
Fuel Capacity: 1409 litres.   **Route Availability:** 6.
Train Supply: Electric, index 38 (electric & diesel).

73961	(73209)		**GB**	GB	GBNR	SE	Alison
73962	(73204)		**GB**	GB	GBNR	SE	Dick Mabbutt
73963	(73206)		**GB**	GB	GBNR	SE	Janice
73964	(73205)		**GB**	GB	GBNR	SE	Jeanette
73965	(73208)		**GB**	GB	GBNR	SE	Des O' Brien

73966–971 have been rebuilt for Caledonian Sleeper but their third rail electric capability has been retained. They have a higher Train Supply index and a slightly higher fuel capacity. Details as 73961–965 except:
Fuel Capacity: 1509 litres.   **Train Supply:** Electric, index 96.

73005 and 73006 were originally assembled at Eastleigh Works.

73966	(73005)	d	**CA**	GB	GBCS	EC
73967	(73006)	d	**CA**	GB	GBCS	EC
73968	(73117)	d	**CA**	GB	GBCS	EC
73969	(73105)	d	**CA**	GB	GBCS	EC
73970	(73103)	d	**CA**	GB	GBCS	EC
73971	(73207)	d	**CA**	GB	GBCS	EC

CLASS 86   BR/ENGLISH ELECTRIC   Bo-Bo

Built: 1965–66 by English Electric Co at Vulcan Foundry, Newton-le-Willows or by BR at Doncaster Works.
Electric Supply System: 25 kV AC 50 Hz overhead.
Traction Motors: AEI 282BZ axle hung.
Maximum Tractive Effort: 207 kN (46500 lbf).
Continuous Rating: 3010 kW (4040 hp) giving a tractive effort of 85 kN (19200 lbf) at 77.5 mph.
Maximum Rail Power: 4550 kW (6100 hp) at 49.5 mph.
Train Brakes: Air.   **Brake Force:** 40 t.
Dimensions: 17.83 x 2.65 m.   **Weight:** 83–86.8 t.
Wheel Diameter: 1156 mm.   **Train Supply:** Electric, index 74.
Design Speed: 110–125 mph.   **Maximum Speed:** 100 mph.
Route Availability: 6.   **Total:** 21.

Formerly numbered E3101–E3200 (not in order).

Class 86s exported for use abroad are listed in section 5 of this book.

Class 86/1. Class 87-type bogies & motors. Details as above except:

Traction Motors: GEC 412AZ frame mounted.
Maximum Tractive Effort: 258 kN (58000 lbf).
Continuous Rating: 3730 kW (5000 hp) giving a tractive effort of 95 kN (21300 lbf) at 87 mph.
Maximum Rail Power: 5860 kW (7860 hp) at 50.8 mph.

Wheel Diameter: 1150 mm.
Design Speed: 110 mph.   **Maximum Speed:** 110 mph.

| 86101 | **IC** | LS | LSLO | CL | Sir William A Stanier FRS |

Class 86/2. Standard design rebuilt with resilient wheels & Flexicoil suspension. Details as in main class heading.

Non-standard livery:

86259 BR "Electric blue". Also carries number E3137.

| 86251 | | **V** | FL | EPEX | CB (S) | |
| 86259 | x | **0** | PP | MBEL | WN | Les Ross/Peter Pan |

Class 86/4. Details as Class 86/2 except:

Traction Motors: AEI 282AZ axle hung.
Maximum Tractive Effort: 258 kN (58000 lbf).
Continuous Rating: 2680 kW (3600 hp) giving a tractive effort of 89 kN (20000 lbf) at 67 mph.
Maximum Rail Power: 4400 kW (5900 hp) at 38 mph.
Weight: 83–83.9 t.
Design Speed: 100 mph.   **Maximum Speed:** 100 mph.

| 86401 | **CA** | WC | AWCA | CS | Mons Meg |

Class 86/6. Freightliner-operated locomotives.

Previously numbered in the Class 86/0 and 86/4 series'. 86608 was also regeared and renumbered 86501 between 2000 and 2016.

Details as Class 86/4 except:
Traction Motors: AEI 282AZ axle hung.
Maximum Speed: 75 mph.   **Train Supply:** Electric, isolated.

86604	**FL**	FL	DHLT	CB (S)
86605	**FL**	FL	DHLT	CB (S)
86607	**FL**	FL	DHLT	CB (S)
86608	**FL**	FL	DHLT	CB (S)
86609	**FL**	FL	DHLT	CB (S)
86610	**FL**	FL	DHLT	CB (S)
86612	**FL**	FL	DHLT	CB (S)
86613	**FL**	FL	DHLT	CB (S)
86614	**FL**	FL	DHLT	CB (S)
86622	**FH**	FL	DHLT	CB (S)
86627	**FL**	FL	DHLT	CB (S)
86628	**FL**	FL	DHLT	CB (S)
86632	**FL**	FL	DHLT	CB (S)
86637	**FH**	FL	DHLT	CB (S)
86638	**FL**	FL	DHLT	CB (S)
86639	**FL**	FL	DHLT	CB (S)

CLASS 87   BREL/GEC   Bo-Bo

Built: 1973–75 by BREL at Crewe Works.
Electric Supply System: 25 kV AC 50 Hz overhead.
Traction Motors: GEC G412AZ frame mounted.
Maximum Tractive Effort: 258 kN (58000 lbf).
Continuous Rating: 3730 kW (5000 hp) giving a tractive effort of 95 kN (21300 lbf) at 87 mph.
Maximum Rail Power: 5860 kW (7860 hp) at 50.8 mph.
Train Brakes: Air.   **Brake Force:** 40 t.
Dimensions: 17.83 x 2.65 m.   **Weight:** 83.3 t.
Wheel Diameter: 1150 mm.   **Train Supply:** Electric, index 95.
Design Speed: 110 mph.   **Maximum Speed:** 110 mph.
Route Availability: 6.   **Total:** 1.

Class 87s exported for use abroad are listed in section 5 of this book.

| 87002 | **IC** | LS | LSLO | CL | Royal Sovereign |

CLASS 88   VOSSLOH/STADLER   Bo-Bo

New Vossloh/Stadler bi-mode DRS locomotives.

Built: 2015–16 by Vossloh/Stadler, Valencia, Spain.
Electric Supply System: 25 kV AC 50 Hz overhead.
Engine: Caterpillar C27 12-cylinder of 708 kW (950 hp) at 1750 rpm.
Main Alternator: ABB AMXL400.
Traction Motors: ABB AMXL400.
Maximum Tractive Effort (Electric): 317 kN (71 260 lbf).
Maximum Tractive Effort (Diesel): 317 kN (71 260 lbf).
Continuous Rating: 4000 kW (5360 hp) giving a tractive effort of 258 kN (58000 lbf) at 28 mph (electric).
Maximum Rail Power:
Train Brakes: Air, regenerative & rheostatic.
Brake Force: 73 t.   **Dimensions:** 20.50 x 2.69 m.
Weight: 85 t.   **Wheel Diameter:** 1100 mm.
Fuel Capacity: 1800 litres.   **Train Supply:** Electric, index 96.
Design Speed: 100 mph.   **Maximum Speed:** 100 mph.
Route Availability: 7.   **Total:** 10.

88001	**DI**	BN	XHVE	KM	Revolution
88002	**DI**	BN	XHVE	KM	Prometheus
88003	**DI**	BN	XHVE	KM	Genesis
88004	**DI**	BN	XHVE	KM	Pandora
88005	**DI**	BN	XHVE	KM	Minerva
88006	**DI**	BN	XHVE	KM	Juno
88007	**DI**	BN	XHVE	KM	Electra
88008	**DI**	BN	XHVE	KM	Ariadne
88009	**DI**	BN	XHVE	KM	Diana
88010	**DI**	BN	XHVE	KM	Aurora

CLASS 90   GEC   Bo-Bo

Built: 1987–90 by BREL at Crewe Works (as sub-contractors for GEC).
Electric Supply System: 25 kV AC 50 Hz overhead.
Traction Motors: GEC G412CY frame mounted.
Maximum Tractive Effort: 258 kN (58000 lbf).
Continuous Rating: 3730 kW (5000 hp) giving a tractive effort of 95 kN (21300 lbf) at 87 mph.
Maximum Rail Power: 5860 kW (7860 hp) at 68.3 mph.
Train Brakes: Air.   **Dimensions:** 18.80 x 2.74 m.
Brake Force: 40 t.   **Wheel Diameter:** 1150 mm.
Weight: 84.5 t.   **Maximum Speed:** 110 mph.
Design Speed: 110 mph.   **Route Availability:** 7.
Train Supply: Electric, index 95.   **Total:** 50.

Advertising liveries:

90024   Malcolm Logistics (blue).
90039   I am the backbone of the economy (black).

90001	b	**IC**	LS	LSLO	CL	Royal Scot
90002	b	**IC**	LS	LSLO	CL	Wolf of Badenoch
90003	b	**FG**	FL	DFLC	CB	
90004	b	**GA**	FL	DFLC	CB	City of Chelmsford
90005	b	**GA**	FL	DFLC	CB	Vice-Admiral Lord Nelson
90006	b	**FG**	FL	DFLC	CB	Modern Railways Magazine/ Roger Ford
90007	b	**GA**	FL	DFLC	CB	Sir John Betjeman
90008	b	**GA**	FL	DFLC	CB	The East Anglian
90009	b	**FG**	FL	DFLC	CB	
90010	b	**FG**	FL	DFLC	CB	
90011	b	**GA**	FL	DFLC	CB	East Anglian Daily Times Suffolk & Proud
90012	b	**GA**	FL	DFLC	CB	Royal Anglian Regiment
90013	b	**GA**	FL	DFLC	CB	
90014	b	**FG**	FL	DFLC	CB	Over the Rainbow
90015	b	**FG**	FL	DFLC	CB	
90016		**FL**	FL	DFLC	CB	
90017		**E**	DB	WQCA	CE (S)	
90018		**DB**	DB	WQAB	CE (S)	The Pride of Bellshill
90019		**DB**	DB	WEDC	CE	Multimodal
90020		**GC**	DB	WEDC	CE	
90021		**FS**	DB	WQAA	CE (S)	
90022		**EG**	DB	WQCA	CE (S)	Freightconnection
90023		**E**	DB	WQCA	CE (S)	
90024		**AL**	DB	WEAC	CE	
90025		**F**	DB	WQCA	CE (S)	
90026		**GC**	DB	WEDC	CE	
90027		**F**	DB	WQCA	CE (S)	Allerton T&RS Depot
90028		**DB**	DB	WQAA	CE (S)	Sir William McAlpine
90029		**GC**	DB	WEDC	CE	
90030		**E**	DB	WQCA	CE (S)	

90031	**E**	DB	WQCA	CE (S)	The Railway Children Partnership
					Working For Street Children Worldwide
90032	**E**	DB	WQCA	CE (S)	
90033	**FE**	DB	WQCA	CE (S)	
90034	**DR**	DB	WEDC	CE	
90035	**DB**	DB	WEAC	CE	
90036	**DB**	DB	WEDC	CE	Driver Jack Mills
90037	**DB**	DB	WEAC	CE	Christine
90038	**FE**	DB	WQCA	CE (S)	
90039	**AL**	DB	WEDC	CE	
90040	**DB**	DB	WQAB	CE (S)	
90041	**FL**	FL	DFLC	CB	
90042	**FH**	FL	DFLC	CB	
90043	**FH**	FL	DFLC	CB	
90044	**FG**	FL	DFLC	CB	
90045	**FH**	FL	DFLC	CB	
90046	**FL**	FL	DFLC	CB	
90047	**FG**	FL	DFLC	CB	
90048	**FG**	FL	DFLC	CB	
90049	**FH**	FL	DFLC	CB	
90050	**FF**	AV	DHLT	CB (S)	

CLASS 91　　　　　GEC　　　　　Bo-Bo

Built: 1988–91 by BREL at Crewe Works (as sub-contractors for GEC).
Electric Supply System: 25 kV AC 50 Hz overhead.
Traction Motors: GEC G426AZ.
Maximum Tractive Effort: 190 kN (43 000 lbf).
Continuous Rating: 4540 kW (6090 hp) giving a tractive effort of 170 kN at 96 mph.
Maximum Rail Power: 4700 kW (6300 hp) at ?? mph.

Train Brakes: Air.	**Dimensions:** 19.41 x 2.74 m.
Brake Force: 45 t.	**Wheel Diameter:** 1000 mm.
Weight: 84 t.	**Maximum Speed:** 125 mph.
Design Speed: 140 mph.	**Route Availability:** 7.
Train Supply: Electric, index 95.	**Total:** 31.

Locomotives were originally numbered in the 910xx series, but were renumbered upon completion of overhauls at Bombardier, Doncaster by the addition of 100 to their original number.

Advertising liveries:

91101 Flying Scotsman (red, white & purple).
91110 Battle of Britain (black and grey).
91111 For the fallen (various with poppy and Union Jack vinyls).

91101	**AL**	E	IECA	NL	FLYING SCOTSMAN
91103	**VE**	E	SAXL	ZB (S)	
91104	**VE**	E	SAXL	ZB (S)	
91105	**VE**	E	IECA	NL	

91106	**VE**	E	IECA	NL	
91107	**VE**	E	IECA	NL	SKYFALL
91108	**VE**	E	SAXL	ZB (S)	
91109	**VE**	E	IECA	NL	Sir Bobby Robson
91110	**AL**	E	IECA	NL	BATTLE OF BRITAIN MEMORIAL FLIGHT
91111	**AL**	E	IECA	NL	For the Fallen
91112	**VE**	E	SAXL	DR (S)	
91114	**VE**	E	IECA	NL	Durham Cathedral
91115	**VE**	E	SAXL	DR (S)	Blaydon Races
91116	**VE**	E	SAXL	DR (S)	
91117	**EX**	EP	EPEX	LR (S)	
91118	**VE**	E	SAXL	DR (S)	The Fusiliers
91119	**IC**	E	IECA	NL	Bounds Green INTERCITY Depot 1977–2017
91120	**EX**	EP	EPEX	LR (S)	
91121	**VE**	E	SAXL	DR (S)	
91122	**VE**	E	EROG	RJ	
91124	**VE**	E	IECA	NL	
91125	**VE**	E	SAXL	DR (S)	
91127	**VE**	E	IECA	NL	
91128	**VE**	E	EROG	RJ	INTERCITY 50
91130	**VE**	E	IECA	NL	Lord Mayor of Newcastle
91131	**VE**	E	SAXL	DR (S)	

CLASS 92   BRUSH   Co-Co

Built: 1993–96 by Brush Traction at Loughborough.
Electric Supply System: 25 kV AC 50 Hz overhead or 750 V DC third rail.
Traction Motors: Asea Brown Boveri design. Model 6FRA 7059B (Asynchronous 3-phase induction motors).
Maximum Tractive Effort: 400 kN (90 000 lbf).
Continuous Rating: 5040 kW (6760 hp) on AC, 4000 kW (5360 hp) on DC.

Maximum Rail Power:	**Train Brakes:** Air.
Brake Force: 63 t.	**Dimensions:** 21.34 x 2.67 m.
Weight: 126 t.	**Wheel Diameter:** 1070 mm.
Design Speed: 140 km/h (87 mph).	**Maximum Speed:** 140 km/h (87 mph).
Train Supply: Electric, index 180 (AC), 108 (DC).	
Route Availability: 7.	**Total:** 33.

* Fitted with TVM430 signalling equipment to operate on High Speed 1.

Class 92s exported for use abroad are listed in section 5 of this book.

Advertising livery: 92017 Stobart Rail (two-tone blue & white).

92004	**EG**	DB	WQCA	CE (S)	Jane Austen
92006 d	**CA**	GB	GBSL	WB	
92007	**EG**	DB	WQBA	CE (S)	Schubert
92008	**EG**	DB	WQCA	CE (S)	Jules Verne
92009 *	**DB**	DB	WQCA	CE (S)	Marco Polo
92010 *d	**CA**	GB	GBST	WB	
92011 *	**EG**	DB	WFBC	CE	Handel
92013	**EG**	DB	WQBA	CE (S)	Puccini
92014 d	**CA**	GB	GBSL	WB	
92015 *	**DB**	DB	WFBC	CE	
92016 *	**DB**	DB	WQCA	CE (S)	
92017	**AL**	DB	WQCA	CE (S)	Bart the Engine
92018 *d	**CA**	GB	GBST	WB	
92019 *	**EG**	DB	WFBC	CE	Wagner
92020 d	**GB**	GB	GBSL	WB	
92021	**EP**	GB	GBSD	LB (S)	Purcell
92023 *d	**CA**	GB	GBSL	WB	
92028 d	**GB**	GB	GBST	WB	
92029	**EG**	DB	WQAB	CE (S)	Dante
92031 *	**DB**	DB	WQBA	CE (S)	
92032 *d	**GB**	GB	GBCT	WB	IMechE Railway Division
92033 d	**CA**	GB	GBSL	WB	
92035	**EG**	DB	WQCA	CE (S)	Mendelssohn
92036 *	**EG**	DB	WFBC	CE	Bertolt Brecht
92037	**EG**	DB	WQCA	CE (S)	Sullivan
92038 *d	**CA**	GB	GBST	WB	
92040	**EP**	GB	GBSD	LB (S)	Goethe
92041 *	**EG**	DB	WFBC	CE	Vaughan Williams
92042 *	**DB**	DB	WFBC	CE	
92043 *d	**GB**	GB	GBST	WB	
92044 *	**EP**	GB	GBCT	WB	Couperin
92045	**EP**	GB	GBSD	LB (S)	Chaucer
92046	**EP**	GB	GBSD	LB (S)	Sweelinck

CLASS 93   STADLER   Bo-Bo

In January 2021 Rail Operations Group placed an order with Stadler for an initial ten Class 93 mixed-traffic tri-mode locomotives, as part of a framework agreement for up to 30 of the type. The locomotive is a development of the DRS Class 88 and as well as having a more powerful diesel engine and electric capability will be fitted with batteries and a slightly higher maximum speed of 110 mph. The locomotives are due to be delivered from early 2023. Full details awaited.

Built: 2021–23 by Stadler, Valencia, Spain.
Electric Supply System: 25 kV AC 50 Hz overhead.
Engine: Caterpillar C32 12-cylinder of 900 kW (1205 hp) at   rpm.
Batteries: Two LTO battery packs providing 400 kW (535 hp).
Main Alternator:
Traction Motors:
Maximum Tractive Effort (Electric):
Maximum Tractive Effort (Diesel):
Continuous Rating: 4000 kW (5360 hp).
Maximum Rail Power:
Train Brakes:

Brake Force:	**Dimensions:**
Weight:	**Wheel Diameter:**
Fuel Capacity:	**Train Supply:**
Design Speed: 110 mph.	**Maximum Speed:** 110 mph.
Route Availability:	**Total:** 10.

93001	RO
93002	RO
93003	RO
93004	RO
93005	RO
93006	RO
93007	RO
93008	RO
93009	RO
93010	RO

3. EUROTUNNEL LOCOMOTIVES

DIESEL LOCOMOTIVES

0001–10 are registered on TOPS as 21901–910.

0001–0005   Krupp MaK   Bo-Bo

Channel Tunnel maintenance and rescue train locomotives.
Built: 1991–92 by MaK at Kiel, Germany (Model DE 1004).
Engine: MTU 12V396 TC 13 of 950 kW (1275 hp) at 1800 rpm.
Main Alternator: ABB.   **Traction Motors:** ABB.
Maximum Tractive Effort: 305 kN (68600 lbf).
Continuous Tractive Effort: 140 kN (31500 lbf) at 20 mph.
Power At Rail: 750 kW (1012 hp).   **Dimensions:** 14.40 x ?? m.
Brake Force: 120 kN.   **Wheel Diameter:** 1000 mm.
Train Brakes: Air.   **Weight:** 90 t.
Maximum Speed: 100 km/h.   **Design Speed:** 120 km/h.
Fuel Capacity: 3500 litres.   **Multiple Working:** Within class.
Train Supply: Not equipped.   **Signalling System:** TVM430 cab signalling.

0001	**GY**	ET	CT		0004	**GY**	ET	CT
0002	**GY**	ET	CT		0005	**GY**	ET	CT
0003	**GY**	ET	CT					

0006–0010   Krupp MaK   Bo-Bo

Channel Tunnel maintenance and rescue locomotives. Rebuilt from
Netherlands Railways/DB Cargo Nederland Class 6400. 0006/07 were
added to the Eurotunnel fleet in 2011, and 0008–10 in 2016.

Built: 1990–91 by MaK at Kiel, Germany (Model DE 6400).
Engine: MTU 12V396 TC 13 of 1180 kW (1580 hp) at 1800 rpm.
Main Alternator: ABB.   **Traction Motors:** ABB.
Maximum Tractive Effort: 290 kN (65200 lbf).
Continuous Tractive Effort: 140 kN (31500 lbf) at 20 mph.
Power At Rail: 750 kW (1012 hp).   **Dimensions:** 14.40 x ?? m.
Brake Force: 120 kN.   **Wheel Diameter:** 1000 mm.
Train Brakes: Air.   **Weight:** 80 t.
Maximum Speed: 120 km/h.   **Design Speed:** 120 km/h.
Fuel Capacity: 2900 litres.   **Multiple Working:** Within class.
Train Supply: Not equipped.

Not fitted with TVM 430 cab signalling so have to operate with another
locomotive when used on HS1. 0010 can only be used for shunting at
Coquelles depot.

0006	(6456)	**GY**	ET	CT		0009	(6451)	**GY**	ET	CT
0007	(6457)	**GY**	ET	CT		0010	(6447)	**EB**	ET	CO
0008	(6450)	**GY**	ET	CT						

0031–0042   HUNSLET/SCHÖMA   0-4-0

Built: 1989–90 by Hunslet Engine Company at Leeds as 900 mm gauge.
Rebuilt: 1993–94 by Schöma in Germany to 1435 mm gauge as Type CFL 200 DCL-R.
Engine: Deutz F10L 413 FW of 170 kW (230 hp) at 2300 rpm.
Transmission: Mechanical Clark 5421-179 type.
Maximum Tractive Effort: 68 kN (15300 lbf).
Continuous Tractive Effort: 47 kN (10570 lbf) at 5 mph.
Power At Rail: 130.1 kW (175 hp).
Brake Force: **Dimensions:** 7.87 (* 10.94) x 2.69 m.
Weight: 25 t. (* 28 t.)   **Wheel Diameter:** 1010 mm.
Maximum Speed: 48 km/h (* 75 km/h).
Fuel Capacity: 450 litres.   **Train Brakes:** Air.
Train Supply: Not equipped.   **Multiple Working:** Not equipped.

* Rebuilt with inspection platforms to check overhead catenary (Type CS 200).

0031		**GY**	ET	CT	FRANCES
0032		**GY**	ET	CT	ELISABETH
0033		**GY**	ET	CT	SILKE
0034		**GY**	ET	CT	AMANDA
0035		**GY**	ET	CT	MARY
0036		**GY**	ET	CT	LAURENCE
0037		**GY**	ET	CT	LYDIE
0038		**GY**	ET	CT	JENNY
0039	*	**GY**	ET	CT	PACITA
0040		**GY**	ET	CT	JILL
0041	*	**GY**	ET	CT	KIM
0042		**GY**	ET	CT	NICOLE

ELECTRIC LOCOMOTIVES

9005–9840   BRUSH/ABB   Bo-Bo-Bo

Built: 1993–2002 by Brush Traction, Loughborough.
Electric Supply System: 25 kV AC 50 Hz overhead.
Traction Motors: Asea Brown Boveri design. Asynchronous 3-phase motors. Model 6FHA 7059 (as built). Model 6FHA 7059C (7000 kW rated locos).
Maximum Tractive Effort: 400kN (90 000 lbf).
Continuous Rating: Class 9/0: 5760 kW (7725 hp). Class 9/7 and 9/8: 7000 kW (9387 hp).
Maximum Rail Power: **Multiple Working:** TDM system.
Brake Force: 50 t.   **Dimensions:** 22.01 x 2.97 x 4.20 m.
Weight: 136 t.   **Wheel Diameter:** 1250 mm.
Maximum Speed: 140 km/h.   **Design Speed:** 140 km/h.
Train Supply: Electric.   **Train Brakes:** Air.

Class 9/0 Original build locos. Built 1993–94.

9005	**EB**	ET	CO	JESSYE NORMAN

9007	**EB**	ET	CO	DAME JOAN SUTHERLAND[1]
9011	**EB**	ET	CO	JOSÉ VAN DAM[1]
9013	**EB**	ET	CO	MARIA CALLAS[1]
9015	**EB**	ET	CO	LÖTSCHBERG 1913[1]
9018	**EB**	ET	CO	WILHELMENIA FERNANDEZ
9022	**EB**	ET	CO	DAME JANET BAKER
9024	**EB**	ET	CO	GOTTHARD 1882
9026	**EB**	ET	CO	FURKATUNNEL 1982
9029	**EB**	ET	CO	THOMAS ALLEN
9033	**EB**	ET	CO	MONTSERRAT CABALLE
9036	**EB**	ET	CO	ALAIN FONDARY[1]
9037	**EB**	ET	CO	

Class 9/7. Increased power freight shuttle locos. Built 2001–02 (9711–23 built 1998–2001 as 9101–13 and rebuilt as 9711–23 2010–12).

9701		**EB**	ET	CO
9702		**EB**	ET	CO
9703		**EB**	ET	CO
9704		**EB**	ET	CO
9705		**EB**	ET	CO
9706		**EB**	ET	CO
9707		**EB**	ET	CO
9711	(9101)	**EB**	ET	CO
9712	(9102)	**EB**	ET	CO
9713	(9103)	**EB**	ET	CO
9714	(9104)	**EB**	ET	CO
9715	(9105)	**EB**	ET	CO
9716	(9106)	**EB**	ET	CO
9717	(9107)	**EB**	ET	CO
9718	(9108)	**EB**	ET	CO
9719	(9109)	**EB**	ET	CO
9720	(9110)	**EB**	ET	CO
9721	(9111)	**EB**	ET	CO
9722	(9112)	**EB**	ET	CO
9723	(9113)	**EB**	ET	CO

Class 9/8 Locos rebuilt from Class 9/0 by adding 800 to the loco number. Uprated to 7000 kW.

90xx and 98xx locomotives have a cab in the blunt end for shunting, except 9840 which does not have this feature.

9801	**EB**	ET	CO	LESLEY GARRETT
9802	**EB**	ET	CO	STUART BURROWS
9803	**EB**	ET	CO	BENJAMIN LUXON
9804	**EB**	ET	CO	
9806	**EB**	ET	CO	REGINE CRESPIN
9808	**EB**	ET	CO	ELISABETH SODERSTROM
9809	**EB**	ET	CO	
9810	**EB**	ET	CO	
9812	**EB**	ET	CO	
9814	**EB**	ET	CO	LUCIA POPP

9816	**EB**	ET	CO
9819	**EB**	ET	CO	MARIA EWING[1]
9820	**EB**	ET	CO	NICOLAI GHIAROV
9821	**EB**	ET	CO
9823	**EB**	ET	CO	DAME ELISABETH LEGGE-SCHWARZKOPF
9825	**EB**	ET	CO
9827	**EB**	ET	CO	BARBARA HENDRICKS
9828	**EB**	ET	CO
9831	**EB**	ET	CO
9832	**EB**	ET	CO	RENATA TEBALDI
9834	**EB**	ET	CO	MIRELLA FRENI
9835	**EB**	ET	CO	NICOLAI GEDDA
9838	**EB**	ET	CO	HILDEGARD BEHRENS
9840	**EB**	ET	CO

[1] nameplates carried on one side only.

4. LOCOMOTIVES AWAITING DISPOSAL

Locomotives that are still extant but best classed as awaiting disposal are listed here.

66048   EMD, Longport Works

5. LOCOMOTIVES EXPORTED FOR USE ABROAD

This section details former British Railways (plus privatisation era) diesel and electric locomotives that have been exported from Great Britain for use in industrial locations or with a main line operator abroad. Not included are locos that are classed as "preserved" abroad. These are included in the Platform 5 "Preserved Locomotives of British Railways" publication.

(S) denotes locomotives that are stored.

Number Other no./name   Location

Class 03

03156		Ferramenta Pugliese, Terlizzi, Bari, Italy

Class 47

47375	92 70 00 47375-5	Continental Railway Solution, Hungary

Class 56

56101	92 55 0659 001-5	FLOYD, Hungary
56115	92 55 0659 002-3	FLOYD, Hungary
56117	92 55 0659 003-1	FLOYD, Hungary (S) Budapest Keleti

Class 58

58001		DB, France, (S) Alizay
58004		DB, France, (S) Alizay
58005		DB, France, (S) Alizay
58006		DB, France, (S) Alizay
58007		DB, France, (S) Alizay
58009		DB, France, (S) Alizay
58010		DB, France, (S) Alizay
58011		DB, France, (S) Alizay
58013		DB, France, (S) Alizay
58018		DB, France, (S) Alizay
58021		DB, France, (S) Alizay
58025		DB, Spain, (S) Albacete
58026		DB, France, (S) Alizay
58027	L52	DB, Spain, (S) Albacete
58032		DB, France, (S) Alizay
58033		DB, France, (S) Alizay
58034		DB, France, (S) Alizay
58035		DB, France, (S) Alizay
58036		DB, France, (S) Alizay
58038		DB, France, (S) Alizay
58039		DB, France, (S) Alizay
58040		DB, France, (S) Alizay
58041	L36	Transfesa, Spain, (S) Albacete
58042		DB, France, (S) Alizay
58044		DB, France, (S) Woippy, Metz

58046		DB, France, (S) Alizay
58049		DB, France, (S) Alizay
58050	L53	DB, Spain, (S) Albacete

Class 66

66022	ECR, France	66202	ECR, France	66237		DBC, Poland
66026	ECR, France	66203	ECR, France	66239		ECR, France
66029	ECR, France	66204	ECR, France	66240		ECR, France
66033	ECR, France	66208	ECR, France	66241		ECR, France
66036	ECR, France	66209	ECR, France	66242		ECR, France
66038	ECR, France	66210	ECR, France	66243		ECR, France
66042	ECR, France	66211	ECR, France	66244		ECR, France
66045	ECR, France	66212	ECR, France	66245		ECR, France
66049	ECR, France	66213	ECR, France	66246		ECR, France
66052	ECR, France	66214	ECR, France	66247		ECR, France
66062	ECR, France	66215	ECR, France	66248		DBC, Poland
66064	ECR, France	66216	ECR, France	66249		ECR, France
66071	ECR, France	66217	ECR, France	66411	66013	FL, Poland
66072	ECR, France	66218	ECR, France	66412	66015	FL, Poland
66123	ECR, France	66219	ECR, France	66417	66014	FL, Poland
66146	DBC, Poland	66220	DBC, Poland	66527	66016	FL, Poland
66153	DBC, Poland	66222	ECR, France	66530	66017	FL, Poland
66157	DBC, Poland	66223	ECR, France	66535	66018	FL, Poland
66159	DBC, Poland	66224	ECR, France	66582	66009	FL, Poland
66163	DBC, Poland	66225	ECR, France	66583	66010	FL, Poland
66166	DBC, Poland	66226	ECR, France	66584	66011	FL, Poland
66173	DBC, Poland	66227	DBC, Poland	66586	66008	FL, Poland
66178	DBC, Poland	66228	ECR, France	66595		FL, Poland
66179	ECR, France	66229	ECR, France	66608	66603	FL, Poland
66180	DBC, Poland	66231	ECR, France	66609	66605	FL, Poland
66189	DBC, Poland	66232	ECR, France	66611	66604	FL, Poland
66191	ECR, France	66233	ECR, France	66612	66606	FL, Poland
66193	ECR, France	66234	ECR, France	66624	66602	FL, Poland
66195	ECR, France	66235	ECR, France	66625	66601	FL, Poland
66196	DBC, Poland	66236	ECR, France	66954		FL, Poland
66201	ECR, France					

Class 86

86213	91 52 00 87703-2 Lancashire Witch	Bulmarket, Bulgaria
86215	91 55 0450 005-8	FLOYD, Hungary
86217	91 55 0450 006-6	FLOYD, Hungary
86218	91 55 0450 004-1	FLOYD, Hungary
86228	91 55 0450 007-4	FLOYD, Hungary
86231	91 52 00 85005-4 Lady of the Lake	Bulmarket, Bulgaria
86232	91 55 0450 003-3	FLOYD, Hungary
86233		Bulmarket, Bulgaria (S) Ruse
86234		Bulmarket, Bulgaria
86235	91 52 00 87704-0 Novelty	Bulmarket, Bulgaria
86242	91 55 0450 008-2	FLOYD, Hungary
86248	91 55 0450 001-7	FLOYD, Hungary
86250	91 55 0450 002-5	FLOYD, Hungary

86424	91 55 0450 009-0		FLOYD, Hungary (S) Budapest
86701	91 52 00 87701-6	Orion	Bulmarket, Bulgaria
86702	91 52 00 87702-4	Cassiopeia	Bulmarket, Bulgaria

Class 87

87003	91 52 00 87003-7		BZK, Bulgaria
87004	91 52 00 87004-5	Britannia	BZK, Bulgaria
87006	91 52 00 87006-0		BZK, Bulgaria
87007	91 52 00 87007-8		BZK, Bulgaria
87008	87008-9		BZK, Bulgaria (S) Ruse
87009	91 52 00 87009-4		Bulmarket, Bulgaria
87010	91 52 00 87010-2		BZK, Bulgaria
87012	91 52 00 87012-8		BZK, Bulgaria
87013	91 52 00 87013-6		BZK, Bulgaria
87014	87014-7		BZK, Bulgaria (S) Sofia
87017	91 52 00 87017-7	Iron Duke	Bulmarket, Bulgaria
87019	91 52 00 87019-3		BZK, Bulgaria
87020	91 52 00 87020-1		BZK, Bulgaria
87022	91 52 00 87022-7		BZK, Bulgaria
87023	91 52 00 87023-5	Velocity	Bulmarket, Bulgaria
87025	91 52 00 87025-0		Bulmarket, Bulgaria
87026	91 52 00 87026-8		BZK, Bulgaria
87028	91 52 00 87028-4		BZK, Bulgaria
87029	91 52 00 87029-2		BZK, Bulgaria
87033	91 52 00 87033-4		BZK, Bulgaria
87034	91 52 00 87034-2		BZK, Bulgaria

Class 92

92001	91 53 0 472 002-1	Mircea Eliade	Transagent Rail, Croatia
92002	91 53 0 472 003-9	Lucian Blaga	Transagent Rail, Croatia
92003		Beethoven	DB Cargo, Romania (S)
92005	91 53 0 472-005-4		Transagent Rail, Croatia
92012	91 53 0 472 001-3	Mihai Eminescu	Transagent Rail, Croatia
92022		Charles Dickens	DB Cargo, Bulgaria (S) Aurubis
92024	91 53 0 472 004-7	Marin Preda	Transagent Rail, Croatia
92025	91 52 1 688 025-1	Oscar Wilde	DB Cargo, Bulgaria
92026		Britten	DB Cargo, Romania
92027	91 52 1 688 027-7	George Eliot	DB Cargo, Bulgaria
92030	91 52 1 688 030-1	Ashford	DB Cargo, Bulgaria
92034	91 52 1 688 034-3	Kipling	DB Cargo, Bulgaria
92039	91 53 0 472 006-2	Eugen Ionescu	DB Cargo, Romania

6. CODES

6.1. LIVERY CODES

Livery codes are used to denote the various liveries carried. It is impossible to list every livery variation which currently exists. In particular, items ignored for this publication include minor colour variations, omission of logos and all numbering, lettering and brandings. Descriptions quoted are thus a general guide only. Logos as appropriate for each livery are normally deemed to be carried. The colour of the lower half of the bodyside is stated first.

AB   Arriva Trains Wales/Welsh Government sponsored dark blue.
AI   Aggregate Industries (green, light grey & blue).
AL   Advertising/promotional livery (see class heading for details).
AR   Anglia Railways (turquoise blue with a white stripe).
AW   Arriva Trains Wales/Welsh Government sponsored dark & light blue.
AZ   Advenza Freight (deep blue with green Advenza brandings).
B   BR blue.
BL   BR Revised blue with yellow cabs, grey roof, large numbers & logo.
CA   Caledonian Sleeper (dark blue).
CD   Cotswold Rail (silver with blue & red logo).
CE   BR Civil Engineers (yellow & grey with black cab doors & window surrounds).
CM   Chiltern Mainline loco-hauled (two-tone grey & silver with blue stripes).
CS   Colas Rail (yellow, orange & black).
CU   Corus (silver with red logos).
DB   DB Cargo (Deutsche Bahn red with grey roof and solebar).
DC   Devon & Cornwall Railways (metallic silver).
DG   BR Departmental (dark grey with black cab doors & window surrounds).
DI   New DRS {Class 68 style} (deep blue & aquamarine with compass logo).
DR   Direct Rail Services (dark blue with light blue or dark grey roof).
DS   Revised Direct Rail Services (dark blue, light blue & green. "Compass" logo).
E   English Welsh & Scottish Railway (maroon bodyside & roof with a broad gold bodyside band).
EA   East Midlands Trains revised HST (dark blue, orange & red).
EB   Eurotunnel (two-tone grey with a broad blue stripe).
EG   "EWS grey" (as **F** but with large yellow & red EWS logo).
EP   European Passenger Services (two-tone grey with dark blue roof).
EX   Europhoenix (silver, blue & red).
F   BR Trainload Freight (two-tone grey with black cab doors & window surrounds. Various logos).
FA   Fastline Freight (grey & black with white & orange stripes).
FB   First Group dark blue.
FE   Railfreight Distribution International (two tone-grey with black cab doors & dark blue roof).
FER   Fertis (light grey with a dark grey roof & solebar).
FF   Freightliner grey (two-tone grey with black cab doors & window surrounds. Freightliner logo).
FG   New Freightliner; Genesee & Wyoming style (orange with black & yellow lower bodyside stripes).

FH	Revised Freightliner {PowerHaul} (dark green with yellow ends & a grey stripe/buffer beam).
FL	Freightliner (dark green with yellow cabs).
FO	BR Railfreight (grey bodysides, yellow cabs & red lower bodyside stripe, large BR logo).
FR	Fragonset Railways (black with silver roof & a red bodyside band lined out in white).
FS	First Group (indigo blue with pink & white stripes).
G	BR Green (plain green, with white stripe on main line locomotives).
GA	Greater Anglia (white with a black stripe).
GB	GB Railfreight (blue with orange cantrail & solebar stripes, orange cabs).
GG	BR green (two-tone green).
GL	First Great Western locomotives (green with a gold stripe).
GW	Great Western Railway (TOC) dark green.
GY	Eurotunnel (grey & yellow).
HA	Hanson Quarry Products (dark blue/silver with oxide red roof).
HH	Hanson & Hall (dark grey with green branding)..
HN	Harry Needle Railroad Company (orange with a black roof and solebar).
HU	Hunslet Engine Company (dark blue & orange).
IC	BR InterCity (dark grey/white/red/white).
K	Black.
KB	Knorr-Bremse Rail UK (blue, white & light green).
LH	BR Loadhaul (black with orange cabsides).
LM	London Midland (white/grey & green with broad black stripe around the windows).
LR	LORAM (red, white & grey).
LW	LNWR (grey with a red solebar).
M	Maroon.
ML	BR Mainline Freight (aircraft blue with a silver stripe).
MP	Midland Pullman (nanking blue & white).
MT	Maritime (blue with white lettering).
N	BR Network SouthEast (white & blue with red lower bodyside stripe, grey solebar & cab ends).
O	Non-standard (see class heading for details).
PC	Pullman Car Company (umber & cream with gold lettering lined out in gold).
RA	RailAdventure (dark grey with light grey cabs and green lettering).
RB	Riviera Trains Oxford blue.
RC	Rail Charter Services (green with a broad silver bodyside stripe).
RL	RMS Locotec (dark blue with light grey cabsides).
RO	Rail Operations Group (dark blue).
RS	Railway Support Services (grey with a red solebar).
RX	Rail Express Systems (dark grey & red with or without blue markings).
RZ	Royal Train revised (plain claret, no lining).
SL	Silverlink (indigo blue with white stripe, green lower body & yellow doors).
SI	ScotRail InterCity (light grey & dark blue with INTER7CITY branding).
SN	Southern (white & dark green with light green semi-circles at one end of each vehicle. Light grey band at solebar level).
ST	Stagecoach (blue with red cabs).
TP	TransPennine Express (silver, grey, blue & purple).
TT	Transmart Trains (all over green).

TW	Transport for Wales (white with a red cantrail stripe and grey lower bodyside stripe).
V	Virgin Trains (red with black doors extending into bodysides, three white lower bodyside stripes).
VE	Virgin Trains East Coast (red & white with black window surrounds).
VN	Belmond Northern Belle (crimson lake & cream lined out in gold).
VP	Virgin Trains shunters (black with a large black & white chequered flag on the bodyside).
WA	Wabtec Rail (black).
WC	West Coast Railway Company maroon.
XC	CrossCountry (two-tone silver with deep crimson ends and pink doors).
Y	Network Rail yellow.

6.2. OWNER CODES

The following codes are used to define the ownership details of the locomotives or rolling stock listed in this book. Codes shown indicate either the legal owner or "responsible custodian" of each vehicle.

125	125 Group	EL	Electric Traction Limited
20	Class 20189	EM	East Midlands Railway
37	Scottish Thirty-Seven Group	EO	ElectroMotive Diesel Services
40	Class 40 Preservation Society	EP	Europhoenix
47	Stratford 47 Group	ET	Eurotunnel
50	Class 50 Alliance	EU	Eurostar International
56	Class 56 Locomotives	EY	European Metal Recycling
70	7029 Clun Castle	FG	First Group
71	71A Locomotives	FL	Freightliner
2L	Class Twenty Locomotives	GB	GB Railfreight
A	Angel Trains	GW	Great Western Railway (assets
AD	AV Dawson		of the Greater Western
AF	Arlington Fleet Services		franchise)
AK	Akiem	HH	Hanson & Hall Rail Services
AM	Alstom	HN	Harry Needle Railroad Company
AV	Arriva UK Trains	HU	Hunslet Engine Company
BD	Bardon Aggregates	HX	Halifax Bank of Scotland
BN	Beacon Rail	LF	Lombard Finance
CD	Crewe Diesel Preservation	LN	London Overground
	Group	LO	LORAM (UK)
CS	Colas Rail	LS	Locomotive Services
D0	D05 Preservation Group	ME	Meteor Power
DA	Data Acquisition & Testing	MR	Mendip Rail
	Services	NB	Boden Rail Engineering
DB	DB Cargo (UK)	NM	National Museum of Science &
DC	DC Rail		Industry
DP	Deltic Preservation Society	NR	Network Rail
DR	Direct Rail Services	NS	Nemesis Rail
DT	The Diesel Traction Group	NY	North Yorkshire Moors
E	Eversholt Rail (UK)		Railway Enterprises
ED	Ed Murray & Sons	P	Porterbrook Leasing Company
EE	English Electric Preservation	PG	Progress Rail UK Leasing

PO	Other private owner	SP	The Scottish Railway
PP	Peter Pan Locomotive Company		Preservation Society
RA	RailAdventure	ST	Shaun Wright
RL	Rail Management Services	SU	SembCorp Utilities UK
	(trading as RMS Locotec)	TT	Transmart Trains
RO	Rail Operations Group	UR	UK Rail Leasing
RS	Railway Support Services	VG	Victoria Group
RV	Riviera Trains	WA	Wabtec Rail Group
RU	Russell Logistics	WC	West Coast Railway Company
SB	Steve Beniston	WM	West Midlands Trains

6.3. LOCOMOTIVE POOL CODES

Locomotives are split into operational groups ("pools") for diagramming and maintenance purposes. The codes used to denote these pools are shown in this publication.

AWCA	West Coast Railway Company operational locomotives.
AWCX	West Coast Railway Company stored locomotives.
CFOL	Class 50 Operations locomotives.
CFSL	Class 40 Preservation Society Locomotives.
COFS	Colas Rail Class 56.
COLO	Colas Rail Classes 66 & 70.
COLS	Colas Rail stored locomotives.
COTS	Colas Rail Classes 37, 43 & 67.
DCRO	DC Rail Class 56.
DCRS	DC Rail Class 60.
DFGI	Freightliner Class 70.
DFHG	Freightliner Class 59.
DFHH	Freightliner Class 66/6.
DFIM	Freightliner Class 66/5.
DFIN	Freightliner low emission Class 66.
DFLC	Freightliner Class 90.
DHLT	Freightliner locomotives awaiting maintenance/repair/disposal.
EFOO	Great Western Railway Class 57.
EFPC	Great Western Railway Class 57.
EHPC	CrossCountry Class 43.
EPEX	Europhoenix locomotives for export.
EPUK	Europhoenix UK locomotives.
EROG	Rail Operations Group electric locomotives.
ERSL	Eastern Rail Services locomotives.
GBBR	GB Railfreight Class 73 for possible rebuilding.
GBBT	GB Railfreight Class 66. Large fuel tanks.
GBCS	GB Railfreight Class 73/9. Caledonian Sleeper.
GBCT	GB Railfreight Class 92. Channel Tunnel traffic.
GBDF	GB Railfreight Class 47.
GBEB	GB Railfreight Class 66. Ex-European, large fuel tanks.
GBED	GB Railfreight Class 73.
GBEL	GB Railfreight Class 66. New build, small fuel tanks.
GBFM	GB Railfreight Class 66. RETB fitted.
GBGD	GB Railfreight Class 56. Operational locomotives.

GBGS	GB Railfreight Class 56. Stored locomotives.
GBHH	GB Railfreight Class 66. Regeared locomotives.
GBLT	GB Railfreight Class 66. Small fuel tanks.
GBNB	GB Railfreight Class 66. New build.
GBNR	GB Railfreight Class 73/9. Network Rail contracts.
GBOB	GB Railfreight Class 66. Former DB Cargo locomotives; large fuel tanks and buckeye couplers.
GBRG	GB Railfreight Class 69.
GBSD	GB Railfreight. Stored locomotives.
GBSL	GB Railfreight Class 92. Caledonian Sleeper.
GBST	GB Railfreight Class 92. Caledonian Sleeper & Channel Tunnel.
GBTG	GB Railfreight Class 60.
GBYH	GB Railfreight Class 59.
GBZZ	GB Railfreight locomotives for disposal.
GROG	Rail Operations Group diesel locomotives.
HAPC	ScotRail Class 43.
HHPC	RailAdventure/Hanson & Hall Class 43.
HNRL	Harry Needle Railroad Company hire locomotives.
HNRS	Harry Needle Railroad Company stored locomotives.
HTLX	Hanson & Hall Rail Services locomotives.
HVAC	Hanson & Hall Rail Services Class 50.
HYWD	South Western Railway Class 73.
ICHP	125 Group Class 43.
IECA	London North Eastern Railway Class 91.
IECP	London North Eastern Railway Class 43 (stored).
LSLO	Locomotive Services operational locomotives.
LSLS	Locomotive Services stored locomotives.
MBDL	Non TOC-owned diesel locomotives.
MBED	Non TOC-owned electro-diesel locomotives.
MBEL	Non TOC-owned electric locomotives.
MOLO	Class 20189 Ltd Class 20.
NRLO	Nemesis Rail locomotives.
QADD	Network Rail locomotives.
QCAR	Network Rail New Measurement Train Class 43.
QETS	Network Rail Class 37.
RAJV	Scottish Railway Preservation Society Class 37.
SAXL	Eversholt Rail off-lease locomotives.
SBXL	Porterbrook Leasing Company stored locomotives.
SCEL	Angel Trains stored locomotives.
SROG	Rail Operations Group stored locomotives
TPEX	TransPennine Express Class 68 locomotives.
UKRL	UK Rail Leasing. Operational locomotives.
UKRM	UK Rail Leasing. Locomotives for overhaul.
UKRS	UK Rail Leasing. Stored locomotives.
WAAC	DB Cargo Class 67.
WAWC	DB Cargo Class 67 for hire to Transport for Wales.
WBAE	DB Cargo Class 66. Locomotives fitted with "stop-start" technology.
WBAI	DB Cargo Class 66. Locomotives returned from Euro Cargo Rail/France.
WBAR	DB Cargo Class 66. Fitted with remote monitoring equipment.
WBAT	DB Cargo Class 66.
WBBE	DB Cargo Class 66. RETB fitted and fitted with "stop-start" technology.

WBBT	DB Cargo Class 66. RETB fitted.	
WBLE	DB Cargo Class 66. Dedicated locomotives for Lickey Incline banking duties. Fitted with "stop-start" technology.	
WBRT	DB Cargo Class 66. Locomotives dedicated to autumn RHTT trains.	
WCAT	DB Cargo Class 60.	
WCBT	DB Cargo Class 60. Extended-range fuel tanks.	
WEAC	DB Cargo Class 90.	
WEDC	DB Cargo Class 90. Modified for operation with Mark 4s.	
WFBC	DB Cargo Class 92 with TVM430 cab signalling equipment for use on High Speed 1.	
WQAA	DB Cargo stored locomotives Group 1A (short-term maintenance).	
WQAB	DB Cargo stored locomotives Group 1B.	
WQBA	DB Cargo stored locomotives Group 2 (unserviceable).	
WQCA	DB Cargo stored locomotives Group 3 (unserviceable).	
WQDA	DB Cargo stored locomotives Group 4 (awaiting disposal or for sale).	
XHAC	Direct Rail Services Classes 37/4 & 57/3.	
XHCE	Direct Rail Services Class 68 for hire to Chiltern Railways.	
XHCK	Direct Rail Services Classes 20 & 57/0.	
XHCS	Direct Rail Services Class 68 for hire to Chiltern Railways (spare locomotives).	
XHHP	Direct Rail Services locomotives – holding pool.	
XHIM	Direct Rail Services locomotives – Intermodal traffic.	
XHNC	Direct Rail Services locomotives – nuclear traffic/general.	
XHSS	Direct Rail Services stored locomotives.	
XHTP	Direct Rail Services Class 68 for hire to TransPennine Express (spare locomotives).	
XHVE	Direct Rail Services Classes 68 & 88.	
XHVT	Direct Rail Services Class 57/3 for hire to Avanti West Coast.	
XSDP	Direct Rail Services locomotives for disposal.	

6.4. ALLOCATION & LOCATION CODES

Allocation codes are used in this publication to denote the normal maintenance base ("depots") of each operational locomotive. However, maintenance may be carried out at other locations and also by mobile teams. The designation (S) denotes stored.

Code	Location	Depot Operator
BH	Barrow Hill (Chesterfield)	Barrow Hill Engine Shed Society
BL	Shackerstone, Battlefield Line	*Storage location only*
BM	Bournemouth	South Western Railway
BO	Bo'ness (West Lothian)	The Bo'ness & Kinneil Railway
BQ	Bury (Greater Manchester)	East Lancashire Railway Trust
BU	Burton-upon-Trent	Nemesis Rail
CB	Crewe Basford Hall	Freightliner Engineering
CE	Crewe International	DB Cargo (UK)
CF	Cardiff Canton	Transport for Wales
CL	Crewe LNWR Heritage	LNWR Heritage Company
CO	Coquelles (France)	Eurotunnel
CR	Crewe Gresty Bridge	Direct Rail Services
CS	Carnforth	West Coast Railway Company

CT	Cheriton (Folkestone)	Eurotunnel
DR	Doncaster Belmont Yard/RMT	*Storage location only*
EC	Edinburgh Craigentinny	Hitachi
EP	Ely Papworth Sidings	*Storage location only*
HA	Haymarket (Edinburgh)	ScotRail
HO	Hope Cement Works	Breedon Hope Cement
HJ	Hoo Junction (Kent)	Colas Rail
KM	Carlisle Kingmoor	Direct Rail Services
KR	Kidderminster	Severn Valley Railway
LA	Laira (Plymouth)	Great Western Railway
LB	Loughborough Works	Brush Traction
LD	Leeds Midland Road	Freightliner Engineering
LM	Long Marston Rail Innovation Centre	Porterbrook Leasing
LR	Leicester	UK Rail Leasing
LT	Longport (Stoke-on-Trent)	ElectroMotive Diesel Services
LW	MoD Longtown (Cumbria)	*Storage location only*
MD	Merehead	Mendip Rail
NC	Norwich Crown Point	Greater Anglia
NL	Neville Hill (Leeds)	Northern
NM	Nottingham Eastcroft	East Midlands Railway/Boden Rail
NY	Grosmont (North Yorkshire)	North Yorkshire Moors Railway Enterprises
PZ	Penzance Long Rock	Great Western Railway
RD	Ruddington (Nottingham Heritage Railway)	125 Group
RJ	Rectory Junction (Nottingham)	Data Acquisition & Testing Services
RR	Doncaster Robert's Road	ElectroMotive Diesel Services
RU	Rugby	Colas Rail
SC	Scunthorpe Steelworks	British Steel
SE	St Leonards (Hastings)	St Leonards Railway Engineering
SL	Stewarts Lane (London)	Govia Thameslink Railway/Belmond
SK	Swanwick West (Derbyshire)	The Princess Royal Locomotive Trust
SW	Swanage	Swanage Railway
TM	Tyseley Locomotive Works	Vintage Trains
TN	Tonbridge	GB Railfreight
TO	Toton (Nottinghamshire)	DB Cargo (UK)
WB	Wembley (London)	Alstom
WN	Willesden (London)	Alstom
WS	Worksop (Nottinghamshire)	Harry Needle Railroad Company
YK	National Railway Museum (York)	National Museum of Science & Industry
ZA	RTC Business Park (Derby)	LORAM (UK)
ZB	Doncaster Works	Wabtec Rail
ZC	Crewe Works	Alstom UK
ZD	Derby Works	Alstom UK
ZG	Eastleigh Works	Arlington Fleet Services
ZI	Ilford Works	Alstom UK
ZJ	Stoke-on-Trent Works	Axiom Rail (Stoke)
ZK	Kilmarnock Works	Brodie Engineering
ZN	Wolverton Works	Gemini Rail Group
ZR	Holgate Works (York)	Network Rail